RESTLESS
ADVENTURE

RESTLESS ADVENTURE

Essays on Contemporary Expressions of Existentialism

ROGER L. SHINN, Editor

PHILIP P. HALLIE

STANLEY ROMAINE HOPPER

ROGER ORTMAYER

ROLLO MAY

CHARLES SCRIBNER'S SONS · NEW YORK

TO

PAUL TILLICH

1886-1965

existential interpreter and

critic of existentialism

A-4.68[V]

PRINTED IN THE UNITED STATES OF AMERICA
Library of Congress Catalog Card Number: 68-12507

CONTENTS

RESTLESS
ADVENTURE

EDITOR'S INTRODUCTION

A Rebellion and Its Career

ROGER L. SHINN

Near the end of *Herzog*, Saul Bellow's popular novel of 1964, Moses Herzog renounces the vogue of "playing at crisis, alienation, apocalypse and desperation." Instead, he will be "loyal to civilization" and "responsible to reason."

That declaration—in the setting of occasional references to Kierkegaard, Heidegger, Buber, and "those German existentialists who tell you how good dread is for you"—appeared to be Bellow's renunciation of existentialism. And certain trend-spotters were quick to announce a turning point in contemporary culture, the end of the existentialist binge that had lured many modern minds far past the point of diminishing returns. The time had come, said the diagnosticians, to recognize a new turn in the history of contemporary culture.

11

Whether the verdict was wishful thinking or an accurate measure of the situation remains to be seen. Before anybody can be sure, a lot of evidence needs to be investigated. But the assumption behind this book is that the faddist stage of existentialism is past or passing, and that for this reason the time is right for an assessing of the existentialist impulse that, far deeper than the fad, has wrought immense consequences in our history.

The thesis of the book is that existentialism is a powerful and complex cultural movement, expressing itself in more human activities than any one specialist can trace. Hence five writers here join their resources to describe how this movement has shaped, shaken, and found expression in their several disciplines.

Note that they are not writing about the *influence* of existentialism *upon* philosophy, theology, literature, art, and psychology—as though existentialism were something outside these areas, moving in upon them and pressing them into its image. An artist, for example, does not read up on existentialism, then apply its ideas to his paintings. It does not matter whether he has ever heard of existentialism. The existentialism *in him*—if he is that kind of artist—becomes visible in his paintings. And his artistic activity makes him an existentialist as truly as his existentialism makes him the kind of artist he is. What happens is that he experiences tremors and commitments, bafflements and certitudes, anxieties and resolutions akin to those experienced by men who write philosophy and theology or try clinically to understand human nature—and by people who rear children, fight or refuse to fight wars, try to relate themselves to society and maintain some kind of integrity in a world that often frustrates their efforts. Such experiences generate the existentialist spirit and expression in contemporary man and his works.

I. NO DEFINITIONS

I have been mentioning existentialism without defining it. And anyone who reads this book, cover to cover, will find that all five writers refuse to define the term. There is something futile, even perverse, about the effort. Existentialism protests against the definitions and categorizations by which men try to simplify life. Almost any self-respecting existentialist refuses to call himself an existentialist. He has to make that refusal. To say, "I am an existentialist," is to say, "I am one of that classification of people known as existentialists"; whereas the existentialist wants to say, "I am myself—and I don't like your effort to fit me into your classifications."

There is another trouble with definition. A precise definition excludes too much, for existentialism is not a precise movement. But a broad definition almost covers the cultural landscape and ceases to have any definitive usefulness. How can one definition include Kierkegaard's passionate faith and Nietzsche's celebration of the death of God—or Sartre's notion that man is "a useless passion" and Buber's sensitivity to the I-Thou relation—or, for that matter, within Sartre alone, the concentration on *nausea* and the affirmation of the dignity of man? Whatever else existentialism means, it means diversity and conflict.

But this is not to say that the word is meaningless. Existentialism is a turbulence set loose in the modern world. A turbulence is real. The air pilot, detecting it through his radar, alerts his passengers to it; they fasten their seat belts and they experience it. But it is hard to define the exact boundaries of the turbulence or to predict its next jolt. Existentialism, a turbulence, is *there*—in our world; and it is *here* —in ourselves. And if we do not know exactly what it is, we feel its impact, and sometimes we need the word to identify it.

The word provides one clue to its own meaning: obviously *existentialism* is coined from the word *existence*. Existentialism turns from abstract essences formed by the mind to the more chaotic stuff of actual existence. It insists that all human observation and understanding are the activities of existing persons, that it is useless and deceptive to claim to understand anything if we remain ignorant of ourselves, and that self-understanding begins not with observing persons but with being a self. Existentialism focuses on concrete, existing realities—the diversified and chaotic stuff of the world and the struggling, striving selves of our experience—rather than upon the abstract ideas that we sometimes mistake for existent reality. It asserts that the actor perceives life more intensely than the spectator, that any speculation detached from involvement gives a fraudulent conception of actual existence.

This kind of concern for existence has a long, sporadic history. We find it in the Bible, which is not a book of doctrines about God but a confessional testimony of a community living with an awareness of God.[1] We find it in Socrates, the gadfly of Athens, the annoying questioner, the thinker—who insists that knowledge must begin with self-knowledge.

Much of subsequent history—political, intellectual, and theological—was preoccupied with the construction of hierarchies of government and hierarchical systems of metaphysics that enclosed the individual, or with the effort of man to manipulate his environment and his fellow men rather than to confront the meaning of his own existence. But in Augustine's *Confessions* the interrogation of personal existence erupted in remarkable intensity. Augustine (354–430), writes

[1] The Scriptures of all the major world religions, unlike books on philosophy of religion and theology, have an unsystematic quality. They include history, anecdotes, poetry, aphorisms. Often their effect is to confront the reader less with a verdict—"Here is what you ought to believe"—than with a question—"What do you make of this?"

William Barrett, "gives us a revelation of subjective experience such as even the greatest Hellenic literature does not, and could not."[2] After Augustine, Christendom managed to contain pretty well this kind of experience within a doctrinal and sacramental structure, although occasional individuals, stimulated either by scriptural tradition or personal experience, took up the highly personal inquiry into existence.

A millennium after Augustine, Martin Luther (1483–1546) did so, with reverberations that shook Christendom. A little later William Shakespeare (1564–1616), especially in *Hamlet* and *King Lear,* raised the disturbing questions about human existence and the universe that were to trouble men for centuries to come. The modern age had arrived. The familiar worldview of the past, the established authorities of religion, metaphysics, and custom were dethroned.

Pascal (1623–62), brilliant scientist and theologian, was the first man to articulate clearly the peculiar dilemmas and paradoxes that were to haunt future generations. A mathematician with the sensitivity of a poet, a theologian at odds with his church, he felt in himself the cleft that was soon to fragment modern culture. He knew the shock of wondering why, in the eternity of time and immensity of space, he was "here rather than there," "now rather than then"[3]—much as Heidegger three centuries later was to describe the experience of being "thrown in" to existence. Pascal wrote: "The silence of these infinite spaces frightens me"[4]—as Camus long after was to echo: "The absurd is born of this confrontation between the human need and the unreasonable silence of the world."[5] Pascal described faith as a wager, with "an eternity

---

2 William Barrett, *Irrational Man* (Garden City: Doubleday, 1958), p. 84.

3 Blaise Pascal, *Pensées* (New York: E. P. Dutton, Everyman's Library), fr. 205.

4 *Ibid.,* fr. 206.

5 Albert Camus, *The Myth of Sisyphus* (London: Hamish Hamilton, 1955), p. 29.

of life and happiness" at stake[6]—as Kierkegaard was later to describe it as a "leap."[7]

But Pascal's fragmentary writings had to wait two centuries for their milieu. First modern man lived through the Age of Reason and the Enlightenment, testing the hope that he would overcome his troubles by the kind of logic and rational skill that actually were deepening the cleft. Then in the nineteenth century the whole achievement was threatened, not because reason failed, but because its very triumphs discovered and constructed a world ever more alien to the vitalities that made human existence joyful or tragic. The romantic movement, first an underground stirring and then an obvious rebellion, shook Western civilization. And somewhere toward one edge of it—not merely a branch of it but not entirely detached from it—existentialism erupted and started its restless adventure.

Despite Pascal and other forerunners, it is customary to date existentialism from Søren Kierkegaard (1813–55). He gave it its initial vocabulary. He combined the anger and the wit, the rational penetration and the distrust of rationalism, the skepticism and the commitment that have since marked existentialism. Only a Kierkegaardian sense of irony could do justice to the fact that this foe of all *isms* should become the father of a new *ism*, that this lampooner of all vogues should set off many vogues. But existentialism is not any ordinary *ism*; it has no way of identifying or counting its adherents, and they are no cozy fraternity but an assortment of individuals who can fight each other as ardently as any outsider.

Existentialism is a rebellion. It is a rebellion for the sake of man against the oppression, the stultification, the bureaucratization, the thing-ification of man. Yet it often seems to

---

[6] Pascal, *Pensées*, fr. 233.

[7] Søren Kierkegaard, *Philosophical Fragments* (Princeton: Princeton University Press, 1944), p. 34.

take a dim view of man in his anxieties and alienation. That is because it aims to deal with *existing* man, not the abstract man who is praised by orators, flattered by politicians, and manipulated by advertisers. Its material is human experience, not the going clichés about experience.

But existentialists, as existing men, are as vulnerable to folly as any men. So these enemies of hypocrisy, posturing, and sloganeering are capable of cultivating their own hypocrisies, postures, and slogans. The man who insists that he is going to be absolutely honest is about to fool somebody—himself or another victim. If existentialism can rid us of much conventional foolishness, it also puts us on guard against its own capacity for foolishness. A radical rebellion should have the courage to question its own excesses and dogmatisms. That is why the authors of this book aim to criticize as well as describe existentialism. All of us, in turn, will be vulnerable to critics who want to point out our follies.

II. FIVE EXPRESSIONS

The five authors of this book might have been four or six or nine; there is no way to number the expressions of existentialism. But five turned out to be as good and convenient a number as any. Certainly it is easy to identify five areas in which the human spirit has worked out expressions of the existentialist impulse. And the sequence of the five chapters makes a kind of sense—although other sequences could likewise be justified.

We lead off in this book with philosophy, because there existentialism is most articulate and there it makes the greatest concessions to the demands of precision. There also we have the best chance of seeing the unity and diversity within its range. Existentialism fits uncomfortably the classifications of academic philosophy, yet cannot be denied recognition among them. Like pragmatism, with which it lives in both

kinship and hostility, it keeps spilling out of the intellec-
tualized world of the university; yet it sometimes incorporates
a strenuous intellectualism in its enterprise. Philip Hallie,
one of the few philosophers equally adept in existentialist
and in analytic philosophies, in esthetics and in logic, writes
the chapter on philosophy.

Our sequence moves from philosophy to theology.
Kierkegaard, the founding father, was a theologian—although
he preferred to call himself a poet or a humorist, and he
cherished his lay status from which he attacked clerical pom-
posity and authority. Existentialism is today more often associated with atheism than with religious affirmation, but it
remains a powerful theological force. My chapter analyzes
the existentialist thrust in theology.

From the beginning most existentialists have said that
their most important messages could not be stated as bald
propositions. Existentialism does not represent a finished
body of thought that can be passed on to a recipient; it requires involvement and fresh discovery from every learner.
Hence most existentialists have experimented with various
forms of discourse, and existentialist communication has
moved through the arts as much as through discursive essays.
This book, therefore, includes a chapter on literature and a
chapter on the visual arts. Literature is verbal, and the existentialist philosophers have often chosen it as their métier.
Thus a philosopher like Sartre deliberately writes novels and
plays to convey his message. But just as often the writer simply does his artistic work, ignorant of or indifferent to any
philosophy called existentialism; then later philosophers discover the existentialist motifs in the art, as scholars have done
with Dostoevski, Hölderlin, and Rilke. Stanley Romaine
Hopper deals with both methods in his description of three
major styles and themes in modern fiction, drama, and
poetry.

The visual artist may be the most existential of all, because in his renunciation of verbal communication he does not compromise by slipping the accepted formulas into his work. As Roger Ortmayer points out, the painter is likely to answer questions about the meaning of his work with the appropriately existentialist response, "What does it mean to you?" Because he does not mouth quotations from Kierkegaard or Heidegger or Sartre, the artist or sculptor may not be identified as an existentialist—and may not care in the least. Yet Ortmayer shows that there are identifiable existentialist qualities in art; for example, the displacement of "aesthetic distance" by involvement or alienation.

Last, for chronological reasons, is the chapter on psychology. Emerging rather recently as an approved discipline and jealous of its status as a science, psychology has often rejected anything so unquantifiable, so resistant to conventional methods of public verifiability, as the affirmations of existentialism. But existentialism is an effort at self-understanding, and psychology tries to understand selves. Hence "existentialist psychotherapy" has entered upon the scene, sometimes as an identifiable school of practice, more often as an unlabeled influence upon psychology. Rollo May, one of the pioneer contributors to the movement, here describes its dynamics and significance.

To these five chapters any reader can add others. The educator, whenever he aims to educate persons rather than simply pour knowledge into minds, whenever he sees in education the elements of discovery and risk and personal appropriation, is something of an existentialist. Modern American education, under the influence of pragmatism, has appropriated existentialist motifs—except when it has substituted too simply goals of growth and socialization for the richer and more complex stuff of human existence. Historiography becomes existential whenever it seeks to probe the relation between freedom and impersonal destiny in the human record. And it enters into typical existentialist questioning when it asks in what ways the historian's own concerns and his own imaginative reliving of the past contribute to his investigations. Modern politics has its existentialist components; for example, the participation of French existentialists in the resistance to Nazism and the strained cordiality of Sartre to the Communists, and the emergence in the United States of the "new left."

Thus the whole history of modern culture has been touched by, and has been part of, the history of existentialism. The five areas selected for this book are perhaps the five most significant; in any case, they offer case studies that may be helpful for modern man's self-understanding throughout his whole experience.

III. COMMUNICATION AND EVALUATION

Each author in this volume faced a problem of communication. Philip Hallie states it in Chapter I. Should he use "vague, enigmatic, and obscure language" to "suggest, remind, offend, cajole, and scandalize" his reader into awareness—the true existentialist mode of communication? Or should he explain and analyze, making precise and explicit distinctions? He and all the other writers did a little of both. All at some points used indirection and suggested what they could not literally say. But, because this is a book *about* existentialism rather than an example of existentialism, all used some straightforward discourse.

By agreement, we followed the convention of dividing each chapter into sections with headings and roman numerals. We hope nobody is deceived. Existentialism can no more be built up out of logical units than a giraffe can be constructed out of cubic building blocks. But clarity is a virtue, even when thinking about an existence that is never entirely clear. So each of us, in his own way, said some things as clearly as he knew how.

Each of us wrote unabashedly in the first person singular,

unafraid of the pronoun "I." Each of us is opinionated, and we made no effort to hide our opinions. Each wrote in his own style and at his own length. There is something hostile to existentialism in suppressing the idiosyncratic person who is doing the writing.

But at the point of expressing opinions, we ran into a common problem—perhaps the most perplexing problem of existentialism. By what criteria were we to evaluate any idea or work of art? Roger Ortmayer states the problem most specifically: existentialist art "has no 'standards' by which it can be evaluated, other than those which inhere in the work itself." Yet existentialism does not justify fraud and hokum. "The artist becomes a totally responsible person—as artist." His responsibility can even be described as "ultimate." But perhaps, says Ortmayer, it is "a weakness of the radical existentialist mode" that "objective criticism is nearly impossible."

The composer, Igor Stravinsky, faced up to this issue when asked how a person today was to recognize "art":

> It is still generally thought of as art if it is shown in a gallery, and as music if it takes place in premises traditionally associated with concerts; which is hardly an answer, but in the absence of identifying rules and conventions, and at a time when an aesthetic object may be anything at all, the "limits of art" are not only airtight but indefinable. As for those who are obliged to keep the racket going, dealers and other middlemen, the formula, "Buy now in the likelihood that it may later turn out to *be* Art" seems to be working very well. Speaking for myself, I could not begin to distinguish music and non-music in some of the concert-hall activity I have observed of late, nor would I be confident of recognizing a new musical genius. In fact, if I were asked to fill Schumann's role today, and hail a new Brahms, I would probably have to modify his dictum to: "Keep your hats on, gentlemen, for all I know he may be a charlatan."[8]

If art is in such confusion, it might be expected that philosophy, with its traditions of criteria for testing truth,

8 Igor Stravinsky, interview in the *New York Review of Books*, June 1, 1967, pp. 14–15.

would be better off. But for existentialism, the important truth is personal truth, untestable by any objective, predefined standards.

Still, no existentialist can leave the issue in total confusion. Existentialists talk about authentic existence and inauthenticity, about accepting and evading responsibility, about good faith and self-deception. With all their moral and artistic differences, existentialists come close to unanimity in recognizing the virtue of acting in freedom, of taking responsibility for decisions, of being and becoming an authentic self.

This is a starting point for judgments—whether moral or philosophical or artistic. Yet it is not enough. The honest, intense zealous person may be incisive or dull, artistically skillful or inept, morally compassionate or fanatical. His personal authenticity does not assure the value or validity of his achievement. That is why Albert Camus found that he had to move from the celebration of the absurd, in *The Stranger* and *The Myth of Sisyphus*, to tragic humanism and sensitivity to human community in *The Plague* and *The Rebel*.

Existentialism belongs to the experience of an age when men live in paradox and tension. It makes judgments that imply standards, although it cannot define the standards. It knows that the best voice is not necessarily the noisiest, but it cannot specify how to recognize the best. It realizes that the most significant freedom is not caprice, but it is unwilling to let any external authority specify the content of freedom. It declares that men must make commitments and test them in action, although it is far from certain what outcomes would vindicate or refute the commitments. To borrow another phrase from Camus, *Exile and the Kingdom*, the title of his final collection of short stories, existentialism knows both exile and intimations of a kingdom of meaning.

That is why this book is called *Restless Adventure*. The five chapters that follow are invitations to follow some of the highways and byways of the adventure.

One

PHILOSOPHY

Indirect Communication and Human Existence

PHILIP P. HALLIE

I. ISOLATION AND COMMUNICATION

Søren Kierkegaard, the Danish father of existentialism, wrote
in his main philosophical work:

> . . . Suppose that it happened to be the view of life of a
> [thinker] . . . that no man ought to have any disciple . . .; suppose
> he also . . . asserted this principle directly, with pathos and unc-
> tion: what would happen? Why then he would be understood; and
> he would soon have applications from at least ten candidates,
> offering to preach this doctrine, in return for a free shave once a
> week. . . .[1]

Kierkegaard thought of himself as a philosopher for whom
"sociability and fellowship" were "unthinkable."[2] Have his

---

[1] Kierkegaard, *Concluding Unscienitfic Postscript*, ed. Walter Lowrie
(Princeton University Press, 1944), p. 70. Henceforward, this work will be
referred to as *CUP*.

[2] *Ibid.*, p. 68n.

disciples, whom we usually call "existentialists," made his ironic joke come true?

The crucial word in the paragraph quoted is the word "directly": it is dangerous for a philosophy such as his, Kierkegaard thought, to be communicated directly. If your philosophy involves regimenting men so that they speak the same words and hold precisely the same beliefs, direct communication might work. But if your philosophy involves awakening people to their own "inwardness," their own "subjective thought," then the laying down of methods and proved, precise conclusions defeats your purpose. What a philosopher of subjectivity needs is *indirect* communication, not a method and a system that demand that we march in lock-step with the Master. It needs metaphors, ironies, laughs, and it needs irritating paradoxes to arouse men. A philosopher of indirect communication must only suggest, must merely occasion the thoughts and feelings of his reader; he must make his reader teach himself, in his own "inwardness." The only disciples Kierkegaard wanted were a little like Socratic followers, men like those who had been jarred by Socrates into reminiscence (*anamnesis*), into independent thought.

A philosophy that suggests, reminds, offends, cajoles, scandalizes men into awareness of their own inward states is rare in Western civilization. We have had for the most part only handy, precise methods, and great systems; these are supposed to be "cogent," that is, are supposed to cog our minds into their movements from premises to conclusions. Indirect communication, in the form of dialogue or metaphor or poetry, does not often serve as an important way of communicating philosophical reflection. And because of the permissiveness of its language, existentialism is one of the most profoundly *diversified* "schools" in the history of Western philosophy. Its conclusions concerning God, say, are sometimes atheistic, sometimes Judaic, sometimes Protestant, sometimes Roman Catholic; and its styles include poems, plays, novels, essays, dialogues, treatises, and even sermons. As a matter of fact, most existentialists have found it quite easy to disown the title "existentialist."

And so the word "existentialism" accumulated meanings with no neat definition within which to work, no authority to keep revisionists in line. But if we take the word broadly to refer to philosophers who have been, according to the philosophers themselves, profoundly influenced by Søren Kierkegaard (and if, of course, we include the Dane himself) we may get at some of the important issues that have been raised under the banner of existentialism. We shall not define the term; we shall try only to get at some of these issues, and at the ways they were raised.

We have already met both an issue and a way of expressing it, when we talked about indirect communication. Existentialists think in terms of indirect communication because they believe, at some crucial juncture in their thought, in what Kierkegaard called "the isolation of inwardness." They believe that it is both possible and necessary to think of a man—at least in certain stages of his life—as isolated from all outside help or pressure. Kierkegaard's greatest philosophic enemy, Hegel, did not believe that such a way of thinking about a man was possible, let alone necessary (if one is being fully rational). And this difference separates the two philosophers and dictates their respective ways of communicating. Man was to be understood as a part of the study of history for Hegel; history was to be understood as a part of the self-awareness of the individual for Kierkegaard. Learning to live *with* pressures from outside one's immediate experience was the great project for Hegel; learning to choose and feel *despite* those pressures was a very great part of Kierkegaard's main project, and a great part of the main project of the other existentialists.

Now before we get much further it is important to notice that isolation and indirect communication are not all there is to existentialism: community and its instrument, direct communication by way of proof, play important roles in the thought of every existentialist from Kierkegaard to Sartre. The point is that the existentialists emphasize isolation and indirect communication more heavily than do most philosophies. This difference—of degree if you will—is their contribution to world thought.

II. A PARABLE FOR EXISTENTIALISM

Imagine yourself in Seville, on the hot pavements of that southern city; it is the sixteenth century, during the time of the Inquisition. Just yesterday a hundred heretics were burned to cinders by order of the Grand Inquisitor. Suddenly Jesus Christ appears on those streets; He mildly moves among the people, giving and receiving love. But the old Cardinal, the Grand Inquisitor himself, wearing his coarse old cassock, passes nearby, and he sees that the people's responsive love is a threat to his own regime. He stands at a distance from that loving throng, and "his eyes gleam with a sinister fire." He points his finger at the center of the throng, and tells his "holy guard" to take Him. They do, and the people bow down to the earth and allow Jesus to be taken from them.

Now it is night in the dungeon of the ancient palace of the Inquisitor. Outside, the fragrance of laurel and lemon floats in the dark and burning air of Seville. The Grand Inquisitor, alone, brings a light into the total darkness of Jesus' prison, and a crucial part of Dostoevski's novel *The Brothers Karamozov*, usually called "The Grand Inquisitor," reaches a new intensity. The old man admonishes Jesus for coming back, for wanting to arouse in the peaceful, obedient minds of his people the "vague, enigmatic, and obscure" forces of disinterested spiritual love. He admonishes Jesus for wanting to arouse men from their orderly, cozy, sheeplike existence under the Inquisitor's rule. He upbraids Him for wanting men to be individuals who cannot be seduced into obedience by an institution that uses bread, clear certainties, and authority to dominate them. He tells Jesus that these poor, weak creatures once thought that they could live by the "free verdict of the heart," without those external supports, but he goes on to tell Him that these same weak creatures learned that they could not bear the uncertainties of initiative, of spiritual independence. They learned that what they wanted most was not to live according to the vague, enigmatic, and obscure language of inwardness; they learned that what they wanted was to give up their independence in exchange for the lucid certainties that visible outward things possess. And so they rebelled against the unpropped freedom Jesus had offered them, and like chicks coming to the warm body of the mother hen, they flocked to the Church and to the Grand Inquisitor. They rebelled against their own obscure inward faith, and submitted to a lucid, outward authority. To achieve community, to be *together*, they gave up the "free verdict of the heart."

The Cardinal admits that he is the ally of that "spirit of self-destruction and non-existence," Satan, who has always tempted men into slavery to a lucid, outward world. But also he insists that he is a friend of these feeble creatures, who need so much support. He is their friend because he wants their happiness; he does not want them to be tortured by the vague promptings of their lonely hearts. He does not love them as Jesus loved them, for their power to make "a free decision for themselves"; he loves them for their weakness, for their need to be happy together, secure, free from want and anxiety. And so not only is his love different from that of Jesus, but also his notion of freedom is different. Here are two radically opposed notions of what a man is and what a man can and should be.

Throughout all these admonitions Jesus keeps silent, listening to this monk who is avowedly an ally of Satan. Then He rises, kisses the bloodless lips of the monk, and, with the Inquisitor's permission, goes back into the dark alleys of the city. But the talk has accomplished nothing, except perhaps to expel Jesus from Seville. He goes on in His way, and the self-sacrificial old man "adheres to his idea."

There are many passages in literature which suggest powerfully the main insights of existentialism. But this "prose-poem" of Dostoevski is surely one of the most rich and comprehensive of these. It was written long after Kierkegaard's death and was in all probability not at all influenced by the writings of the Dane. And so I am not proposing Dostoevski as an existentialist philosopher. I offer it only as an emblem or a parable of the complex notions of freedom and rebellion that are to be found in existentialist literature. The conflict between the "fearful burden of free choice" and "the quiet humble happiness of weak creatures" is perhaps the basic theme of existentialism. And what better way is there to express a philosophy that so heavily employs indirect communication than by a "prose-poem" that keeps Jesus silent but still makes him as eloquent as his antagonist!

But the intent of this chapter involves more than the presentation of parables; its intent is to discuss the "philosophy" of existentialism, and the word "philosophy," as I have been saying, means primarily detailed analysis and careful syntheses—at least here in the West. I am by training something of an "analytic" philosopher, one given more to telling or proving than to suggesting or arousing. So I have been torn by two desires: to present existentialism by way of indirect communication, "vague, enigmatic, and obscure" language, and to bring to bear upon it some precise and explicit distinctions that will help put it more squarely in the context of Western philosophizing. In the conviction that I shall fail to satisfy at least one of these desires and possibly both, I find this consolation: the failure may be instructive, especially for those who wish to look more carefully at the writings of the existentialists.

To put the parable, then, into more literal terms, we can say that (1) there are two different doctrines of rebellion in the Grand Inquisitor prose-poem, and (2) there are two different doctrines of freedom. Christ's kind of rebellion is against a peaceful community of submissive creatures governed totally by an external authority; the Grand Inquisitor's rebellion is against the vague, enigmatic, and obscure Good News of Jesus, which amounted to a kind of unworldly madness because it left each of these poor creatures to his own feeble devices. Christ's sort of man was free from all outward pressures, and made decisions for himself in "vague, enigmatic, and obscure" language; the Grand Inquisitor's kind of man was free of the anxiety that lonely independence brings. Christ's man was the inward, spiritual man; the Inquisitor's man was the outwardly oriented, happy man.

From what has been said before, it should be plain that Christ's man is far closer to existentialism than is the Inquisitor's. The existentialists are against the reification of man, against pushing him around in public institutions or in philosophic systems as if he were a thing or a gregarious animal; and they are trying to awaken people to making for themselves what Dostoevski called the "free verdict of the heart" in anxiety and in solitude.

But such words as "rebellion" and "freedom" might suggest to the reader that the existentialists are offering a political philosophy. This is not the case. They are not advocating a particular sort of government which allows individuals to make choices for themselves. Existentialists do not think about institutions, except to attack them. They think in terms of one person at a time, an individual in his inwardness, and in his relationships to *his* experienced world. Their main interest is in the way things appear to an individual, *not* in the way things work from the point of view of a government.

III. EXISTENTIALISM AND THE HISTORY OF PHILOSOPHY

In the course of giving some literal meaning to terms like "rebellion" and "freedom," it will be useful to see existentialism's relationships with various traditions in the history of philosophy—especially since these traditions do concentrate on giving literal meaning to their terminology.

Many philosophers have taken man's inward awareness of emotion, choice, and thinking itself as the basis of all reliable knowledge. In some of the dialogues of Plato, in the works of St. Bonaventure, Descartes, Rousseau, Bergson, and Whitehead, among others, you will find the conviction that those who establish belief on external sense experience (philosophers like Hobbes, Hume, and the modern logical positivists) fail to establish it on a secure foundation. These philosophers of inward experience talk about the external world around them, but only after they have taken full account of that entity with which we have immediate, intimate contact, ourselves. And to them the existentialists are closely related.

Still another tradition in the history of philosophy is that of wisdom-philosophizing. There are some philosophers who are far more interested in human realities, or in helping people to cure themselves of spiritual maladies like fanaticism, cowardice, superstition than they are in constructing an objective philosophy of nature. Some of these men, like Epictetus and Marcus Aurelius (who were both Stoics), thought that such a definitive account of nature could be constructed, but instead of devoting their lives to doing this, they turned their attention primarily to solving the pressing spiritual problems of men. Epictetus emphasized the Stoic

distinction between things in our control (like our own attitudes and choices) and things outside our control (like the
laws of physical nature), then asked men to confine themselves to controlling what they could control and not disquiet-
ing themselves over what they couldn't. This distinction,
incidentally, occurs throughout the history of existentialism
at crucial points, but the existentialists use it to stir men up
rather than to make them "Stoical." Still other wisdom-
philosophers, like the Greek skeptics and the French skeptic
Montaigne, had their doubts about the possibility of devising
a unified, final science, and they used these doubts to dis-
courage men from straying beyond their personal, living
everyday experience. Kierkegaard in his *CUP* speaks knowl-
edgeably and well of the Greek skeptics, and he himself used
doubt as a laxative for purging men (the Greek skeptics were
doctors, and the wisdom-philosophers are therapists of the
human spirit) of any pretense to having a superpersonal
knowledge of ultimate reality. The true skeptic, Kierkegaard
saw, was somebody who used doubt only to make men attend
to "phenomena," their own living experience, rather than to
high-flown, would-be scientific systems. The true Greek
skeptic stops doubting when he has made men suspend judgment on ultimate reality and spend their lives in their own
proximate experience. This emphasis on phenomena, and for
reasons sometimes close to skepticism, is an important element of existentialism.

When, long after Kierkegaard's death, Husserl developed what was called the "phenomenological" approach,
which said *"Epecho"* ("I suspend judgment") on causes beyond or "behind" appearances, the existentialists found his
approach very congenial indeed. The skeptics and Kierkegaard had long ago been telling men to mind their own experience. But again, it is wrong to think of existentialism as
a modern kind of skepticism: the ultimate desideratum for
skeptics (as for Stoics) was tranquility. And tranquility is for

pigs, sheep, and hens, according to the existentialists, not for existing men.

And so various philosophic traditions help us to place and understand existentialism in the history of Western philosophy, despite its profound differences from the majority of Western philosophies. But there is one tradition we have only mentioned whose influence on Kierkegaard is broader and deeper than any we have discussed here. It has to do with the Socratic doctrine of reminiscence, or *anamnesis*. Socrates taught men, so this doctrine goes, not mainly by rote or by proofs, but by reminders, suggestions, questions that made his students come to their own conclusions and become new creatures.[3] He made them realize their own ignorance and find truths for themselves, and thus be reborn. He was a midwife helping a student to give birth to his own new personality by having him know himself more lucidly, more explicitly. All of these aspects of Socrates' teaching, including his use of irony in order to do these things, are important parts of Kierkegaard's philosophy and of the philosophies of his followers. Reminiscence, self-knowledge, rebirth—all of these are what Kierkegaard thanks Socrates for in his brief work *Philosophical Fragments*. And so might more recent existentialists thank this man who would not hawk knowledge wholesale in the streets of Athens, but would establish relationships between particular individuals for the purpose of helping the individual to find his own way through his own experience. Because Kierkegaard believed in all these Socratic doctrines (which I have loosely summarized at the outset of this chapter under the rubric "indirect communication") he wrote in his *Philosophical Fragments* (p. 44): ". . . between man and man the Socratic relationship is the highest and truest. . . ."

[3] *Philosophical Fragments or a A Fragment of Philosophy*, Søren Kierkegaard, ed. David F. Swenson (Princeton: Princeton University Press, 1946), p. 13.

Of course, Kierkegaard believed in a paradoxical, Christian God, and Socrates did not; and there are many other important points of disagreement between the Socrates Plato presents to us and the Kierkegaard we know. But to understand existentialism in the context of the history of Western thought we must look further than the wisdom philosophers or the philosophers of inward experience—we must look at that ugly, ironic, trouble-making questioner, Socrates. The analogy between the father of existentialism and the father of Western philosophy is not a superficial one.

IV. EXISTENTIALISM, REBELLION, AND FREEDOM

1. *Rebellion*

All existentialists believe that solitude has an important role to play in man's rebellion against being treated like a thing and in man's freedom to make his own choices; and all believe that communication between these solitary beings is an important part of their rebellion and freedom. Moreover, all of them have debts to Socrates in particular and the wisdom philosophers, as well as to the philosophers of inward experience, in general. But if you want to understand the rich texture of existentialist thought, you must get more specific.

Rebellion is negative and destructive, whatever else it may prove to be. And existentialism has the spirit of rebellion about it. Existentialists are usually better at ridiculing or humiliating something than they are at constructing a positive, detailed program. True, some existentialists, like Heidegger and Sartre, are more positive and systematic than others, but rebellion is central to the tone and content of even these philosophies.

Fundamentally, what they are rebellious against is man's

tendency to become obsessed with objectivity. The outward objects men encounter and the disinterested contemplation of those objects so fascinate men that they ignore or explain away their own intense feelings in terms of those coolly contemplated objects. Kierkegaard, for instance, believed that "man is potentially spirit"[4] and that this spirit is actualized by our passionate choices. And he believed that objectivity, looking at things as if our own lives were not passionately involved in them, is the way of living that keeps these potentialities dormant.

It is because the felt relationship a person experiences with his world is so important to the existentialist that he uses indirect communication so much. And it is because the intensity of that felt relationship is the measure of a man's existence that the existentialists try to induce that intensity in us by paradox, satire, irony, and all the other devices of indirect communication. They are trying to wake us up, not trying to lead us along by the halter of objectivity like sleepy horses.

Men fall under this temptation to objectivity in two ways: theoretically and practically. In science and systematic metaphysics, on the one hand, and in institutional practice, on the other, men reveal their obsession with what Dostoevski called "non-existence."

As far as their rebellion against systematic theory is concerned, it consists in the main in a long, sneering laugh at the absentmindedness of certain philosophers. Hegel and the Hegelians, for instance, spent their lives piecing together their great system, and as a result their minds were absent from their living. Indulging themselves in idle speculative curiosity, they built castles in the air, while they slipped and fell in the slime of their own intimate, unguided everyday lives. Their existence as particular individuals, their choices in everyday life or in crises were beneath them as philoso-

[4] *CUP*, p. 221.

phers. Their essentially idle (objective) curiosity made them patient with working on vast, unfinished systems; what they were doing was not as important to complete as a good meal, and so they could patiently speak of passing the torch of truth on to future generations; dead to practical self-interest, and therefore "dead to spirit and enthusiasm"[5] they could spend their lives *approaching* the truth, without any decisiveness, without ever stopping the infinite process[6] of accumulating and piecing together objective truths. And so they were laughably unaware of their own all-important, powerful needs, and of the abyss between these needs and their abstract, disinterested systems.

This abyss is so deep that the existentialists usually do not try to refute the objectivists by any objective proofs (though again Heidegger and Sartre come closer to doing this than do any other existentialists). For instance, Kierkegaard did not think that he could march across a Bridge of Disproof from Hegel's system to his own philosophy. Like the skeptics, he believed that you get all tangled up in an "objective" system if you attack it frontally, and on its own terms. He believed that such criticism is tedious, indeed interminable; both sides can multiply reasons and counter-reasons until their defenders die, unredeemed. No. So great is the gap between objectivity and subjectivity for existentialists that no proofs can move between them. What you do with a Hegelian system, according to Kierkegaard, is draw from your "fund of humor."[7] If you are involved in the system, leap out of it, giving it the horse-laugh over your shoulder; and by that gesture you may arouse others to leap out of it for themselves.

And Sartre, in his book *Being and Nothingness*, turns his back on the scientists who would tell us how environment

5 *Ibid.*, p. 180.
6 *Ibid.*, p. 102.
7 *Ibid.*, p. 34n.

and physiology determine a man's actions; he does not try
to disprove their scientific studies in general or in detail. He
simply proclaims, in passing,[8] that "the ultimate term of . . .
existential inquiry must be a *choice*. . . . It thereby abandons
the supposition that the environment acts mechanically on
the subject under consideration." He simply states that he
will confine his study to the way things appear in particular
situations, and he assumes that for existential inquiry "no
objective description of this environment could be of any use
to us."

The difference, the deep split between objects as treated
by science or metaphysical systems and subjects as intensely experienced by themselves, is the beginning of all existentialism.

And in between the father of existentialism and the
youngest of its present leaders you find the same division.
For instance, Martin Heidegger, who directly influenced
Sartre, speaks of it in terms that remind us of his love for
the Black Forest of southern Germany. He says that there are
certain paths men take in their efforts to get to the center of
the forest of Being, paths which thin out and soon get lost in
the underbrush; these are the *Holzwege*, the vanishing paths,
the dead-ends of man's efforts to understand the universe.
One of these, the most traveled, is the disinterested scientific
study of external objects, the study of resemblances between
things. The "forms" of Plato, the "essences" of Aristotle, the
"universals" of the Medievals, and the refined mathematical
formulas of modern science are instances of man's fascination
with generality, resemblances. The reasons for this fascination are not hard to find: man wants to master his world, to
manipulate it, and in order to do so he must know what to
expect from certain events; he expresses these expectations
in generalizations. But Heidegger urges us to turn our back
on this vanishing path into abstraction; he urges us to dis-

[8] Jean-Paul Sartre, *Being and Nothingness*, trans. Hazel Barnes (New
York: Philosophical Library, 1956), p. 572.

cover in our intimate, particular experience the Being that wells up from within us, from our roots in nature (again the forest metaphors).

Gabriel Marcel, the French Catholic existentialist, divides "problem-solving" from "mystery-recognizing," and Karl Jaspers, the German who, unlike Heidegger, estranged himself from Nazism, sees the break as one between *Verstand* or scientific understanding and *Selbstsein* or the total grasp of the universe that one experiences in pain, guilt, and dying. And Camus, the French atheist, puts it this way in *The Myth of Sisyphus*:

> That universal reason, practical or ethical, that determinism, those categories that explain everything are enough to make a decent man laugh. They have nothing to do with mind. They negate its profound truth.[9]

The absurdity of life for Camus and for other existentialists consists in the fact that our intimate experience is one thing and these laws, these systems, these generalities are another. As Camus puts it: ". . . all true knowledge is impossible. Solely appearances can be enumerated and the climate make itself felt."[10] Existentialists, as we have noticed, do not try to disprove particular claims to objective knowledge; they simply describe the way life feels from the inside of our emotion-soaked, particular experience. And occasionally they comment on the fact that a scientific or objectivistic substitute for this feeling is out of the question, nonsense.

But I have been treating this rebellion as purely theoretical, as directed against the exact sciences and objectivistic metaphysics. As our Parable implies, the existentialists' rebellion is also against the institutions that attempt to reify men, that generalize or organize them into machines that move impersonally, objects driving objects in mechanical

9 Albert Camus, *The Myth of Sisyphus*, trans. Justin O'Brien (New York: Alfred A. Knopf, 1955; Vintage Books), p. 16.

10 *Ibid.*, p. 9.

sequence. Kierkegaard called such an organization "Christen-dom"; Camus thought of this conspiracy against human existence as the bureaucracy of the mind and the heart. But all of them say that any institution that makes men uniform, powerless, and predictable is an agent of nonexistence, a force that in practice commits the same error that the objectivistic sciences commit in theory: the error of confusing outward uniformity with inward particularity, the being of things with the existence of conscious men.

It has become necessary now to look more closely at the differences between the types of rebellion proposed by various existentialists. Let us divide the existentialists into two sorts: the Wedding-existentialists, and the Divorce-existentialists. And let us explain this distinction by saying that the Wedding-existentialists believe in a deep communion with the nonhuman world that surrounds man; they believe that there is hope, as far as man's realizing his own deepest desires, in this enfolding reality. It is a hope, of course, that objective science cannot help us to realize—only intimate experience can do this, only the choices men make by "the free verdict of the heart." On the other hand, the Divorce-existentialists have no such hope for ultimate communion between man and the nonhuman world that surrounds him. They see struggle and inevitable defeat at the center of the relationship between man and nature. On the one hand, they see the brutal indifference of nature to man's desires and, on the other, they see creatures doomed to fall prey eventually to that indifference. The Wedding-existentialists are usually described as "religious"; among them are the Protestant Kierke-gaard, the Jew Buber, the Catholic Marcel, and the somewhat difficult to classify German Wedding-philosophers, Jaspers and Heidegger. And indeed, even the classifications "Protestant," etc., are hard to apply to thinkers so recalcitrant to institutional uniformities. The Divorce-existentialists are

usually thought of as atheists; among them are Camus and
Sartre.

They share the existentialists' distaste for confusing men
with things, but of course the particular forms their rebellions take have a great deal to do with whether they have any
hope for ultimate reconciliation with the nonhuman world
that surrounds and penetrates them. All of these men find at
the center of subjectivity or intimate experience the phenomenon of choice; they all find that each moment of life
involves a choice that cannot be rationally justified, and that
is so important that our existence or our nonexistence hinges
on it. They all want us to avoid the sloth, timidity, and ir-
responsibility that come from thinking of ourselves as part
of some natural or social bureaucracy where the buck is
always being passed to something or somebody else who is
supposed to have "caused" my choice, or "ordered" it. In
short, they are all defenders of solitude.

But for the Wedding-existentialists, as the term implies,
this solitude is temporary and superficial. They will not let
themselves be swallowed up in scientific or institutional
bureaucracies, but the ultimate purpose of all *their* rebellion
against these is to free men's wills so that they may choose to
recognize the mystery (Marcel's language) of spiritual and
divine existence. This recognition of the mystery takes various forms among the Wedding-existentialists: the solitary
sacrifice of reason that occurs when we believe in a flat, absolute contradiction, when we believe that an all-powerful,
eternal God died suffering on a cross (Kierkegaard), the decision to see in pain, suffering, and dying the presence of an
enfolding love in the universe (Jaspers), and so on.

But the Divorce-existentialists see the others as escapists,
as men unwilling to face the ongoing, lonely struggle of
perpetual choosing; they see them as timid, sentimental, obscurantist. The only lucid course of thinking for men, according to Camus, for example, is that which allows one to

face vigorously, independently, and without hope the inevitable "opposition, laceration, and divorce"[11] between the rest
of nature and man. For the Divorce-existentialists, mysteries,
enfoldings, absolute paradoxes are philosophical suicide, the
self-destruction of man's capacity to see experience for what it
plainly is before the lights are turned out by the old escapist
language. And the accusation of ignoring or obscuring *phenomena* is, as we have seen, a very serious one to make
against an existentialist.

And so we can say that in addition to rebelling against
the enemies of existentialism, objective reason and coercive
institutions, the existentialists attack the positions of each
other as far as the ultimate hopelessness of life is concerned.
For instance, Jaspers attacks a technological society which
makes men live lives of desire, envy, and ultimately hopeless
anonymity. He does not want men to think of themselves
as finite things that resemble each other and resemble ani-
mals on a basic biological level. He attacks such a society
because in it men choose to live in their flesh instead of living
in full awareness of a Whole which enfolds each creature in
a vast love. But for Camus, the various sorts of bureaucrats
are not fully existent because they do not see clearly that
men are only finite beings and do not ceaselessly struggle
against the faceless indifference of the natural world. They
do not see that they are doomed to die in a desert. These are

---

11 *Ibid.*, p. 26. After *The Myth of Sisyphus*, Camus seemed to take somewhat more kindly to nature. Swimming, for instance, became an important
symbol of spiritual refreshment to him. A few months before his death I
spoke with him in his office at his publisher's building, and he told me that
he was even more weary than ever of his notion of a nature empty of human
values. He said that he was translating Dostoevski and others not only because
he wanted to do this work but also to pass the time till his confidence that
nature supports some human values would ripen. He said that he was grop-
ing for a vocabulary that would help him make nature an occasional ally.
But his sudden death in an automobile accident prevented whatever wedding
he might have brought about. Just when he was trying to see nature as an
ally he was indifferently killed.

two quite different kinds of rebellion because they terminate in two quite different kinds of confrontations with the rest of the natural world.

Such deep differences have made many students of Kierkegaard (or students of his students) disclaim the label "existentialist." But if we wish to find some significance in the movement as a whole, we must find it in their shared enmity toward those bureaucrats of mind and heart who see man as the kind of creature who is functioning best when he is so tangled up in scientific and institutional red tape that he cannot act on his own and cannot be held responsible for his choices.

2. *Freedom*

Now we come to the term which in various forms has been the nerve of our comments on existentialism: freedom. In most philosophies that assert the "freedom" of man, universal determinism is refuted in some way or another. That is, arguments are put forward to show that there is a break in the causal "chain," a break that comes just before the will of man acts. For other defenders of freedom, freedom is defined as (to use Whitehead's phrase) the "practicability of purpose," the power to do what one wishes to do. One does not bother to think of causal "chains." One thinks only about visible, tangible chains. As we have seen in various ways, the existentialists do not refute causal determinism; they simply turn their backs on the causal, objectivistic study of man and nature. They are willing to admit that such a study culminates in what Sartre and Camus call "universal determinism." But they are not interested in such a study—it is too abstract for them, too general. To locate one's choices in such a study is, as Kierkegaard puts it,[12] like trying to find one's way from one Danish town to another by using a map of Europe on

12 *CUP*, p. 275.

which Denmark shows no larger than a steel penpoint. Or rather it is even more impossible than this.

And so the existentialists are more interested in how freedom feels than in how some abstract study can refute or redeem it. But this does not make them defenders of freedom as the power to do what one wishes to do. If such freedom were important to them, they might well be more friendly to the technological applications of pure science which help us do many things we want to do. And they might even be friendly to institutions that teach us to wish to do the right thing, and then help us to do it in exchange for our undying gratitude. No. Freedom is a deeper, different thing from doing what one wishes to do; freedom for the existentialists consists in man's power to make himself and to determine the meaningfulness of his universe. They believe that the choices a man makes make the man.

Both sorts of existentialists believe in the distinction between initial choice and consequent choice. An initial choice or a basic choice directly influences the lesser or consequent choices he makes. For example, one can choose a deliberative, calculating life, and this basic choice determines one's way of living; one then does not leap before one looks, but rather looks long and then tries not to leap at all. Or one can opt for a life of obedience to authority, whether that authority be governmental, customary, or the pressure of physical drives; in this case, one's initial choice has again minimized one's spontaneity, and has made one part of a complex machine. In the language of Sartre's major philosophic work, the first volume of which was published in 1960,[13] such basic choices make us part of the "practico-inert." They put us in a position of, again to use Sartre's language, "serial powerlessness," buck passing, feeling that our own particular decisions will make no difference, will change nothing, and are not really ours anyway. On the other hand, we can choose a

[13] *Critique de la raison dialectique* (Paris: Gallimard, 1960).

full awareness of our power to give goals to our lives, and we can assume full responsibility for our actions. As Orestes puts it in Sartre's *The Flies*, Act III: "I am a man, and every man must blaze his own trail." That trail is his way of life, his essence, *what* he is, what his consequent choices are.

To put it another way, freedom for the existentialists is that which all men have, the power to choose their goals; but it is a power which can undermine itself, which can enslave us. In *Either/Or*, Kierkegaard shows how Don Giovanni, in Mozart's opera, is a musical idea which represents a force in nature, pushed by sexual drives, rebuffed or gratified by circumstances. But he is a slave of forces he has not willed; he is a body in nature with no spiritual force of his own. Kierkegaard hears Mozart's overture to the opera as not only a celebration of the Don's gaiety but a dirge over his deep dread of being less than a fully free man, less than a man whose choices make unimportant to him the push and pull of natural forces. Now contrast the Don with Kierkegaard's Judge William, who also appears in *Either/Or*. The judge has chosen to be in command of himself despite nature and society; he has chosen to marry, and to be faithful in the depths of his being to the vow he made before God and man in the wedding ceremony. In sickness and in health, no matter what the circumstances, he will keep his vow; he is his vow; his vow is his way of life, clearly known to him, to his wife, and to God. In his initial freedom he chose consequent freedom from natural circumstances. In Kierkegaard's *Fear and Trembling* the Knight of Faith, by crucifying his finite, rational powers on the Absolute Paradox, frees himself most completely from bondage to finite, natural things.

I am tempted to simplify at this point in a way that will carry us more deeply into the existentialists' notions of freedom: freedom is, to use the language of Stoics, self-control. All men have it basically, in their intimate experience, but some men choose to give it up. The "Bad Faith" of Sartre is man's choice (always unsuccessful) to become a thing, a tool,

a machine in the hands of others. For Camus to become a
bureaucrat of the mind or the heart involves the same deadly
voluntary loss of self-control. In fact, all I have been saying
about rebellion applies here. The existentialists are saying
that men may choose to give up control of themselves to
nature or circumstance—as did the weak flock of the Grand
Inquisitor; or they may choose to rebel against the pressures
of nature and make their choices in defiance of these pressures—as Jesus advocated in His silence.

But this brings us again to the important difference between the Wedding-existentialists and the Divorce-existentialists. For the Divorce-existentialists this self-control, this
awareness of the principles of one's own action, is never
given up until nature kills us. The lucid awareness that I,
as an individual, contribute whatever meaning there is in
this blank, indifferent desert world accompanies the Divorce-
existentialist to his grave. Only in the self-control that does
not surrender to the sloth, timidity, postponement, or senti-
mentality that many men fall into does full existence lie for
thinkers like Sartre and Camus.

But for the Wedding-existentialists, man's initial freedom is basically his power to choose between an exclusive
concern for the world of finite things and a faithful awareness
of an enfolding Love or Being or Mystery. The Wedding-
existentialists believe that all men must live in the world of
daily struggle, but they also believe that men may also live—
if they wish the fullness of freedom and existence—in *submission* to the infinite. For them self control vis-à-vis nature
has as its climax and justification submission to infinite being. They are the reconciled ones, who find in nature ciphers,
traces, hints that men may read and thereby learn the ultimate meaning of it all. Behind the blank, brutal face of nature they feel a redemptive force to which we can hopefully
give ourselves.

The Divorce-existentialists believe that the fullest freedom lies in man's power to live without hope or excuse or

external justification; in the lucid awareness of each moment they find the only salvation there is. As Sartre puts it, "all human activities are equivalent . . . and . . . all are on principle doomed to failure."[14] To make this point clear, he goes on to say that the solitary drinker is superior to the leader of nations if the drinker sees his goal clearly and accomplishes it with no shilly-shallying, while the leader is agitated and unclear about his goals and their realization. The solitary drinker is the freest, the most fully existent man. But the most fully existent man, the freest man, for the Wedding-existentialist is the man whose every act has been quickened by his felt relationship to the infinite, whose rebellions terminate in loving surrender to what is deeper and more lasting than human goals.

These profound differences amongst the existentialists should not obscure the fact that for all sorts of existentialism the moment of initial choice is a lonely one, involving no guidance from rational considerations or calculations. Only a certain type of initial choice brings these considerations into play. All existentialists in this crucial moment (which recurs throughout one's life) have their backs turned to the facts and generalizations of the social and natural sciences. And this, the existential moment, is the center of all their concerns, however they may differ among themselves as to the value of making one choice rather than another. Somewhere Gabriel Marcel, speaking for all the existentialists as he so often does, has written that "in a sense everything always starts from zero." In this sense all men are free from the past and from nature and from God at the recurring moments of initial choice, according to the existentialists.

V. SKETCH OF A CRITIQUE

Many of the criticisms of existentialism do not make contact with their object—they are stands that in the end

14 *Being and Nothingness*, p. 627.

look as arbitrary as the stands they are attacking. The philosophers who believe in the ultimate victory of science and technology over all human problems, and who attack existentialism for its "vague, enigmatic, and obscure" language fail to make contact, as Kierkegaard says in *CUP*,[15] because they have "nothing in common with what is under attack." Evocation and invocation are forms of address they do not attach much "meaning" to, and so from the beginning their various charges of something like "irrationalism" do nothing but show how happy they themselves are with the content and promises of everyday speech and scientific work. Perhaps this is all only fair, since the existentialists do much the same sort of thing to the defenders of scientific optimism. But surely we must make a distinction between criticisms that are question-begging and self-congratulatory, and criticisms that are going to try to move our thought forward. Progressive criticism is not like love, which, they say, is blind; but it is not like hate either, which is blinder still. It is perhaps more like compassion, which, of course, can be humiliating enough for its object. In this small space let me suggest two criticisms that have something in common with what is under attack.

The first is that the existentialists seem to be frustrating their own important ideal, subjectivity, when they tell us so much about what we should do and should not do. For instance, Kierkegaard in his *CUP*[16] tells us that he himself is "making absolutely no demands" upon the reader—the reader is free to make his own choices. And their attacks on proof, on direct communication as something that "binds all in obedience under the sway of the . . . philosopher . . ."[17] convey this same sense of not wanting to lay down laws for the reader. But look at Kierkegaard's claims revolving around

15 *CUP*, p. 112.
16 *Ibid.*, pp. 125, 127, *passim.*
17 *Ibid.*, p. 122.

his basic assertion[18] that "every human being is essentially spirit"; *only* riskful choice can actualize these potentialities, *not* formulas, evidence, or other external pressures—it is all up to our subjectivity. But nobody has defined more single-mindedly than Kierkegaard himself the requirements that *must* be fulfilled if one is to be a Christian (and no one has described more precisely than the atheistic existentialists what it means to fail or to succeed at existing). Much of existentialism is dogmatism in disguise, direct communication masquerading as indirect communication; they tell us what is the case concerning the essence of man—or they argue with each other about that essence, that is, try to tell each other what is the case. In either instance they are far from making "absolutely no demands" upon the reader—they are often offering new strait-jackets with one hand, while with the other they take off the strait-jackets of the Establishment.

In Act III of *The Flies*, Zeus tells Electra that she is a mere child, that she never seriously willed to do evil, poor lonely creature; he tells her that she toyed with dreams of murder "because that's a game to play alone." And Electra, weakling that she is, victim of direct communication, of external pressure, says, "I'm beginning to understand." But Orestes, who is struggling to achieve Good Faith, responsibility for his freedom, chastises his sister in the spirit of Sartre himself:

> Listen, Electra! Now you are condemning yourself.
> Who except yourself can know what you really desired?
> Dare you let another decide for you?

And this is typical of Sartre's sensitivity to Bad Faith, to letting others treat one like a machine of their own construction. But Sartre himself, not only in his biographies of people like Baudelaire and Genet, but also in general in his phenomenological ontology, is doing just what Zeus was doing

18 *Ibid.*, p. 233.

to Electra, and he is wanting *us* to do just what Electra was getting ready to do. He is telling us the structures of our lives. In detail that is at least as great as Freud's or Marx's determinism he is telling us the structure of our being which is independent of our own choices; he is telling us an objective truth about our intimate experience. In short, no matter how hard existentialists try to exorcise objectivity or detailed external pressures upon man's free choice, no matter how often they tell us that *we* choose our essence, the fact is that they in their various ways have chosen our essences for us, even as other objectivist philosophers have done. To the degree that they do anything more than arouse us to follow the "free verdict of the heart," *they* lay down that verdict for us in as much detail as other dogmatic philosophers do.

But this criticism is not as far-reaching as the second. The whole tendency of existentialism is to make us think of choices as starting from zero, as we have suggested. As we have been noticing all along, they usually see choice as something separate from or in defiance of what science or even common sense might think of as "reasons" or "causes" for choice. And this split between choice and any basis of choice sometimes approaches the ridiculous. We have noticed this remark from *Being and Nothingness*:

> . . . existential inquiry . . . abandons the supposition that the environment acts mechanically on the subject under consideration. The environment can act on the subject only to the exact extent that he comprehends it. . . . Hence no objective description of this environment could be of any use to us.

And in saying these things, Sartre speaks for all existentialists, as I have tried to indicate. But surely this claim is either question-begging or wrong. What about a hammer-stroke on the head? Does this not act mechanically on the subject? Will a man who has chosen fortitude fall more slowly from a smashed skull than one who has chosen timidity? Stroke for stroke a brave man goes down as heavily under a sledge ham-

mer as does a coward, even though both do not "comprehend" the stroke.

Of course, what lies behind Sartre's remarkable but
characteristic claim is the *epoche* of the phenomenologist,
which urges us to restrain from talking about somatic or
metaphysical causes of experience. But what was once a suspension of judgment has now become a positive claim concerning the effects of environment on experience, and this
claim neither Sartre nor any other existentialist who says experience starts from zero can defend, or even tries to defend.
Of course, they could begin such a defense by *defining* "environment" in such a way as to be totally independent from
the meaning of the word "comprehension" or "subject"—but
this would be a thin verbal victory, and would empty of all
empirical reference the whole idea of a break between experience and nature.

The existentialists from the beginning exclude all possible environmental or somatic causes from any explanation
of human choice. But not all "objective description" is deadly
to choice or freedom. Surgery, anesthesia, and many other
medical techniques have helped to make existence as a living
person possible for many people. The existentialists would
tell us that Helen Keller chose to understand; but the fact
is that she was also helped in this choice by bodily actions
and by various objective techniques. Choice can make a man
what he is, but willing and environment come together to
make up his choice; or if they don't, at least man must act
as if he believes this if he is to make a Helen Keller come into
a fuller existence. By separating environmental forces from
choice the existentialists have fragmented and obscured our
understanding of the forces that come together to make a fully
aware person. They have by this question-begging, unques-
tioning exclusion polarized the scientific optimists against
them, and have hindered the person's understanding of the
texture of choice.

But causes of choice are not all they exclude without defense. They exclude reasons too, or when, as in Kierkegaard, they mention them, they denigrate them as threats to freedom, to spontaneity. Consider a passage from the life of Caesar in Plutarch's *Lives*.[19] The existentialist would emphasize one part of the passage, and ignore the rest; the circumspect man, following Plutarch himself, would look at the whole passage. The scene is the crossing of the Rubicon; Caesar is in the process of deciding whether to do it and thus initiate civil war between himself and Pompey. This is the passage an existentialist would pick as a description of his decision:

> . . . in a sort of passion, casting aside calculation, and abandoning himself to what might come, and using the proverb frequently in their mouths who enter upon dangerous and bold attempts, "The die is cast," with these words he took the river.

The riskful choice, the anguish, the familiar elements of existentialist choice are here. But, as a matter of fact, there is more—there is Caesar, the calculating, rational man. And here is a somewhat fuller account of his momentous decision:

> When he came to the river Rubicon, which parts Gaul within the Alps from the rest of Italy, his thoughts began to work, now he was just entering upon the danger, and he wavered much in his mind when he considered the greatness of the enterprise into which he was throwing himself. He checked his course and ordered a halt, while he revolved with himself, and often changed his opinion one way and the other, without speaking a word. This was when his purposes fluctuated most; presently he also discussed the matter with his friends who were about him . . . computing how many calamities his passing that river would bring upon mankind, and what a relation of it would be transmitted to posterity. At last, in a sort of passion. . . .

---

[19] Plutarch, *The Lives of the Noble Grecians and Romans*, trans. John Dryden, and rev. Arthur Hugh Clough (New York: Random House, Modern Library), p. 874.

And then the passage ends existentialistically. In my opinion, the greatest weakness in existentialism is that it is not faithful enough to the phenomena of choice—it does not show the whole of an important decision, and leads us to believe in not only the causelessness but also the reasonlessness of decisions. From the Rubicon decision it leaves out the author of the *Gallic Wars* and the *Commentaries,* and presents us only with a man "casting aside calculation." But the whole man crossed the Rubicon, and his calculations were part of his decision. There is an old Hungarian saying that goes: "The whip cracks at the tip."[20] A decision culminates in "a sort of passion," but the tip is not all there is to a whip—there is a handle and a stalk. Existentialism has an overwhelming tendency to ignore these and see only the cracking tip. It is not faithful enough to the whole phenomenon of choice. It is too eager to put into Caesar's mouth a remark that that formidable general could never utter: ". . . no objective description . . . could be of any use." Its distrust of objectivity is so great that it often fails to see how intimately involved it is with subjectivity.

VI. CONCLUSION

These remarks are not meant to be a refutation of existentialism. No well-developed philosophy has ever been acknowledged by its defenders to be "refuted." Every rich philosophy has ways of absorbing and responding to adverse criticism. These remarks are signposts indicating what I believe are the necessary future developments of existentialism. Sartre in his massive philosophical work-in-progress, *Critique de la raison dialectique,* may well contribute to these developments in the later volumes of that work. But if the existen-

20 I am grateful to Mrs. Magda Polanyi for telling me this proverb in this crisp language.

tialists' replies to such criticisms start getting shrill or far-fetched, it is likely that existentialism will become one more ruin on the Appian Way to the Eternal Truth, one more abandoned philosophy.

For it is plain that the existentialists' sharp break between subjectivity and objectivity obscures and ignores human experience as much as it illumines this experience. Objective considerations demand and get entry into the center of our lives; and it is likely that anybody who tries to abandon them or explain them away will be abandoned himself.

But this too is clear: if you ignore the presence and the force of man's riskful choices, if you ignore the crack of the whip, you will not make these intimate experiences go away either, and you may well condemn your philosophy to sterility and irrevelance. The existentialists, using the direct and indirect powers of language, have tried to widen the course of the history of philosophy to include emotion-laden human experience amid the "data" of philosophy; surely, trying to explain away or ignore that experience is as quixotic as trying to explain away or ignore objective considerations. Objective calculation and subjective passion temper each other in the lives of all of us, and must temper each other in our philosophies.

Two

THEOLOGY

The Prodigal Son of Biblical Faith

ROGER L. SHINN

Existentialism is a prodigal son of biblical faith. Often this son wanders in far countries, devouring all the delicacies and husks of contemporary life. Sometimes he returns to home and father. Coming back to his family, this son meets both the welcome of the father and the hostility of the elder brother. Perhaps he deserves both.

Existentialism is always restless. This prodigal son can never be entirely happy in his parental home, because he cannot settle into any tradition. Certainly he cannot let his ancestors make his decisions for him. His family, likewise, can never be entirely comfortable with him. He is too disconcerting, too rebellious to fit into any household.

Yet his rebellion is part of a family quarrel. Even when he hates his father it is with a son's hatred. He cannot deny

53

his ancestry. He may be Søren Kierkegaard on his deathbed, refusing the sacrament from the pastor who was his boyhood friend, yet trusting in Christ. Or he may be Jean-Paul Sartre, rejecting God, Christ, and all that sacred tradition stands for, yet unable to ignore his heritage as in his writing he creates Christ-figures and deliberately parodies scriptural faith. Always this son is both heir and rebel.

I. EXISTENCE AND BIBLICAL FAITH

Since existentialism is concerned with what is, not with what might rationally be conceived, there is little point in wondering whether it might have arisen on nonbiblical soil. The fact is that, whether in trust or in rejection, in devotion or in antagonism, existentialism has its origins in biblical faith.

In its pilgrimage existentialism has occasionally found affinities with oriental religion. Inquirers have discovered significant resemblances with Indian and Chinese thought,[1] and some existentialists have found a cultic fascination in Zen Buddhism. Certainly existentialism will never be chained to any one heritage. It welcomes insights wherever it can find them. But its concern with concrete existence, in all its factuality and contingency, means that it cannot join wholeheartedly the classic oriental quest, which continuously abstracts from experience for the sake of reaching a goal beyond particularity.

Within the Western tradition existentialism looks to those sources which recognize the uniqueness of things and events rather than the uniformities of patterns. Its concentration is not on the ordered and hierarchical world, on "the great chain of being" elaborated by so much of metaphysics.

[1] See, e.g., William Barrett, *Irrational Man* (Garden City: Doubleday & Co., 1948), pp. 51–52, 252–233. Also K. Guru Dutt, *Existentialism and Indian Thought* (New York: Philosophical Library, 1960).

It is, rather, concerned with the world where chaos impinges on meaning, where nature is less an ordered system than a dynamic power that is both promise and threat. It lives in a history where radical doubt faces God, not in the clarity of rational understanding or the transcendence of a mystical vision, but in a dying man on a cross.

Existentialism derives from *existence*. And in its concentration on existence is its deep kinship with biblical ways of thinking. I am quite aware of the irony of "systematizing" existentialism or fitting it into any neat pattern, but once the folly of any such procedure is recognized, there can be no harm in pointing out three aspects of this kinship.

First, we can look at Kierkegaard's complaint against philosophy's penchant for building systems. His famous protest asserted that a system of philosophy is possible but not a system of existence. This existing world meets us in its overwhelming variety. We know its concrete reality through our senses as well as our minds. Each object in it is different from all others. The rational enterprises of science and philosophy find this variety too bewildering to comprehend. So they deliberately look past concrete existence for the essences that may be rationally conceived and systematized. By this method they attain their imposing accomplishments. But in so doing they make a foolish mistake if they confuse their constructions for existing reality.

Kierkegaard, it is often argued, was hostile to science and has nothing worth saying to a scientific age. Occasionally, it is true, his polemical statements seem to express a withering contempt for science. But the more noteworthy point is that contemporary scientists, in their own conception of their work, are usually closer to Kierkegaard than to the science and philosophy that he attacked. Many of them (in the tradition of Whitehead) regard their work as dealing with abstractions, which are valuable for understanding but must never be confused with the concrete reality of objects and events.

Even more of them (the operationalists) claim only a functional validity for their concepts and hypotheses, which may be worked out with the utmost experimental precision but which are certainly not the same as the richness of existence.

The constant confrontation with existence takes us back to the Bible, where men claimed little understanding of the world but lived in it with a vivid awareness. The existentialist is like Job, wondering at the wild horse, the crocodile, the hippopotamus. (Today Picasso looks at the horse and bull in a comparable way.) These are living creatures, not concepts. They are beautiful and terrifying. One cannot fit them into the orderly hierarchy of being. They are alien to man, yet akin in the kinship of all creation. They have nothing to do with human purposes. One can learn about them but hardly "understand" them—whatever that might mean. One can exult in them, fear them, wonder at them. They *exist*.

But if all things exist, it is *personal existence* that we know directly. Here is the second major affinity between existentialism and biblical thought. An immediate issue of all living is self-awareness, self-confrontation. Again Kierkegaard offers the primary example, as he ridicules the systematic philosophers who try to answer all the world's profound questions without even asking the fundamental one, Who am I? Indeed their concern to answer the other questions may be their means of evading the more tormenting one.

Many existentialists reserve the term "existence" for *personal existence*, denying its relevance for impersonal objects. Others do not cultivate that particular vocabulary. But all raise pointed questions about personal existence, about the nature of selfhood, about self-discovery in decision and action. Whatever we know about the world, each of us knows most immediately that part of it which is himself. And the self is the biggest problem for each of us. So all understanding and all living require us to confront this self.

That is why Kierkegaard so admired Socrates, the gadfly

of Athens. The existentialist affection is not for Plato with his metaphysical speculations but for Socrates, the relentless questioner, the disturber of men's minds, the resolute martyr. Yet the existentialist self-understanding is more biblical than Socratic. It asks the biblical questions about man's freedom, his anxiety, his loneliness and his need for others, his guilt, his relation to his creator (or his relation to being and nonbeing), his death. The existentialist, like the psalmist, looks at the stars and asks, "What is man?" He hears Jesus say, "Do not be anxious about your life," and wonders what this means when anxiety is part of selfhood. He recognizes the constant scriptural call to decision and realizes that living is deciding. He responds to the biblical promise of freedom, knowing that men often praise freedom even while they dread it.

The third specific kinship between biblical faith and existentialism concerns the awareness of history and faith in God. Among the religions of the world biblical faith places a radical emphasis upon the relation between God and history. All mature religion rejects the notion that God is simply another among the many existing objects in the world. On this issue the biblical polemic against idolatry is as harsh as anything comparable in human literature. Then, however, a different issue arises. Once religion rejects the identification of God with any finite object, it faces the question of religious epistemology or of revelation. Here one characteristic method is to insist that, since God by nature and by definition is universal, men apprehend Him by dissociating Him from the particular, by letting their minds move from the specifics of experience to the transcendent. If they reason from experience to God, they must reason from the most universal experiences and the most general data. Whether the path be through nature or through mysticism whether God be transcendent or immanent, one apprehends Him by getting away from the particular to the universal.

But at just this point biblical faith is primarily neither

natural nor mystical but historical. The universal God is known in concrete historical experience. To recognize God is not to move *from* existence but *into* existence.

The prophetic faith of the Old Testament makes a series of affirmations on this issue. It delivers its smashing attacks upon idolatry. It declares a transcendent God, yet continuously points to His activity in a specific history—especially the particular acts of the Exodus. Whenever people make an exclusive claim upon this God, prophetic faith reasserts His universality. He is the God of the Exodus, yet also the God who has raised up other peoples and their leaders. Thus this God is universal. But to know Him, the prophet does not so much generalize upon universal history as point to concrete episodes in Israel's historical existence.

In the New Testament the focus is again historical existence in the specific event of Jesus the Christ. As the Jew remembers the Exodus, the Christian remembers Golgotha and Easter. But against any attempt to particularize God, the New Testament declares that Christ is the act of the universal God who seeks to save all men—Jew and Samaritan, Greek and Ethiopian. In Christ there is neither Jew nor Greek, bond nor free. In Him the universal *Logos*, through whom everything was created, enters into human history. Yet the Christian best recognizes the God and Father of Jesus Christ not by generalizing from all historical data but by entering intensively into the specific concrete history in Galilee and around Jerusalem "under Pontius Pilate."

Thus biblical faith appeals to concrete historical existence. The contrast with most philosophical theisms is obvious. If the philosopher follows the Kantian analysis, in which to exist is to be subject to the forms of perception (time and space), the philosopher may deny that God *exists*. He is pure essence or beyond the distinction between essence and existence. One can say that He is, that He is the source of existence, but not that He enters into existence. By contrast biblical faith (though innocent of this philosophical vocabulary) declares in effect that the uncreated God not only is creator of all existence but furthermore enters into the historical existence of His people in time and space.

Biblical faith is thus radically existential in its perception of God, as we have already found it to be in its view of the world and man. Although it protests against deification of any existing object, it asserts that God reveals Himself in historical existence. The atheistic existentialisms of our time are an authentic echo of the biblical protest against idolatry. Theological existentialism is biblical both in its protest against idolatry and in its affirmation of existential, historical revelation.

II. RADICAL FAITH

The pioneer figure in modern existentialism, the man who impressed himself and his ideas on the whole movement, is Søren Kierkegaard, the Danish philosopher and lay theologian who lived from 1813 to 1855. Kierkegaard made no claim to invention of a new philosophy. He recognized his own background in Socrates and the Bible. Behind him lay a long tradition of Christian existentialism (without the name) in Augustine, Luther, and Pascal (see pp. 14–16). The German romantic movement fed into his consciousness. But despite his spiritual ancestors and contemporaries, he was a strikingly original thinker. He coined the vocabulary, threw out the challenges to outsiders, and set the terms of the quarrels among insiders that have marked existentialism to this day.

As a Christian, Kierkegaard's vocation was to show the radical nature of faith, to show it, in true existentialist manner, by both his writings and his career. Whether writing from outside the faith or inside it—he did both—he insisted that Christianity was not for spectators but for doers. It was a call for utter trust, thorough commitment, all-out discipleship.

The issue of Christianity is not to learn the correct Christian doctrines. It is, rather, the question, "How can I become a Christian?" If the antithesis were between doubt and belief, one might move smoothly through a spectrum: complete uncertainty, recognition of possibility, acceptance of probability, assertion of very high probability, complete acceptance. But, says Kierkegaard, the antithesis is between despair and belief, between offense and trust, between defiance and commitment. There is no way to make the gap easy to cross. In our fear and trembling, we are called to radical faith. Such faith demands that we "venture far out," that we cast ourselves on 70,000 fathoms of water. No one can simply reason himself into a faith that by its nature is not the acceptance of a probable hypothesis but a risky venture.

Kierkegaard calls the process the "leap of faith." This is not to say that it is an emotional binge, a violent lurch of the passions. Granted, this faith is absurd. But the absurd is not the silly. In mathematics the square root of minus 1 is a surd, an irrational number, but it is far from meaningless. Faith is absurd because it deals with the irrationalities inherent in living. It is a response to what Camus, without believing, calls "the dazzling God of Kierkegaard."[2] It is commitment of the total self, not of mind or emotion alone.

For such faith there is no persuasive reason apart from faith. How can there be? To give such a reason is to appeal for faith on behalf of something else, which then is obviously the more basic object of faith. If, to take a common example, someone commends belief in God as a support for social stability, obviously the real god is social stability.

The effect of this Christian existentialism is, then, to strip faith of all external supports. As trust in God, faith

2 Albert Camus, *The Myth of Sisyphus* (London: Hamish Hamilton, 1955) p. 43.

depends only on God. It needs and wants nothing else. The meaning of this sheer independence of faith becomes clear when we look at some of its specific qualities. I shall here state them in their radical Kierkegaardian form. Later I shall return to some of the problems they pose.

1). Faith seeks no support in natural theology or rational metaphysics. It wants none of the classical arguments that seek to prove (or nowadays, more often, show the plausibility) of the reality of God.

Partly the reason is philosophical. The logical theories of existentialism are akin to those of traditional nominalism, which is skeptical of the classical proofs. Its sensitivity to the unique and chaotic elements in existence is stronger than its respect for the orders and hierarchies that give force to the proofs. Its skepticism questions the assumptions behind all the metaphysical systems. So existentialism usually finds logical flaws in natural theology.

But the violent anger of a Kierkegaard goes much further. The arguments for God are not only a logical fraud: they are also a blasphemous distortion of faith. "Fear and trembling signifies that a God exists—a fact which no man and no established order dare for an instant forget."[3] To stand off and balance coolly the arguments about God's existence is to miss the whole meaning of man's relation to God. In a characteristic explosion Kierkegaard writes:

> So rather let us sin, sin out and out, seduce maidens, murder men, commit highway robbery—after all, that can be repented of, and such a criminal God can still get a hold on. But this proud superiority which has risen to such a height scarcely can be repented of, it has a semblance of profundity which deceives. So let us mock God, out and out, as has been done before in the world—this is always preferable to the disparaging air of importance with which one would prove God's existence. For to prove the existence of one

3 Søren Kierkegaard, *Training in Christianity*, trans. Walter Lowrie (Princeton: Princeton University Press, 1944), p. 89.

who is present is the most shameless affront, since it is an attempt
to make him ridiculous; but unfortunately people have no inkling
of this and for sheer seriousness regard it as a pious undertaking.
But how could it occur to anybody to prove that he exists, unless
one had permitted oneself to ignore him, and now makes the thing
all the worse by proving his existence before his very nose? . . .
One proves God's existence by worship . . . not by proofs.[4]

2). Just as faith seeks no support from natural theology,
so it wants none from history. But here the matter is far more
complex, because of the Christian belief in historical
revelation.

On one issue any argument from history is exactly comparable to the arguments from nature. General history tells
us nothing about God. Kierkegaard directs his thrusts at
his many contemporaries, especially Hegel, who saw the
movement of history as evidence of God. Today, when the
nineteenth-century faith in progress is largely blasted, Kierkegaard's argument is more persuasive and less shocking than
when he set it forth.

If Christian faith is thus independent of general history,
it is nevertheless a response to the specific history of God's
deed in Christ. In a paradoxical world this is the absolute
paradox: that the eternal God should enter into time, and
that man should base an eternal consciousness and eternal
happiness upon a point in time. In this sense alone faith
depends completely upon history—upon a single historical
event.

But this historical event is unknown to the normal processes of historical research. History sees in Christ only an
unimpressive man—a poor and humble person, lacking all
the pomp of achievement and the trappings of majesty. He
is rumored to be born of a virgin, but is more probably of
illegitimate birth. He has nothing, commands no power. He

4 Søren Kierkegaard, *Concluding Unscientific Postscript*, trans. Walter
Lowrie (Princeton: Princeton University Press, 1941), p. 485.

dies as a criminal, obviously unprotected by God. He is an utterly unlikely candidate for divinity. Faith, not history, sees here the doing of God.

Every attempt to support faith by digging out historical evidence about Jesus is futile, since all the evidence is as likely to refute faith. The miracles, often used to sustain faith, are obviously improbable. The testimony of the past is unpersuasive by the canons of historical evidence. Only faith sees the reality hidden in the evidence. It can find no support and wants no support from the accumulation of objective data. Hence Kierkegaard frames his famous sentence:

> If the contemporary generation had left nothing behind them but these words: "We have believed that in such and such a year God appeared among us in the humble figure of a servant, that he lived and taught in our community, and finally died," it would be more than enough.[5]

If this is "more than enough," one might ask what would be just barely enough. But Kierkegaard's point is that "the most voluminous account can in all eternity do nothing more." For no quantity of fact can make faith easier or more significant.

Kierkegaard's skepticism is more radical than Hume's in the preceding century, but its meaning is quite different. Kierkegaard does not neatly balance the probabilities and therefore doubt. Having taken the offense of Christ, he can easily take the lesser offenses that go with Christian belief. But he frees faith from dependence on its accoutrements. No one who has learned from Kierkegaard will find his faith jolted by doubts concerning historical details.

Similarly Kierkegaard—though it was never his intention —takes the sting out of biblical criticism. The critical study of the Bible, already an activity of scholars in his time, hit

5 Søren Kierkegaard, *Philosophical Fragments*, trans. David Swenson (Princeton: Princeton University Press, 1936), p. 87.

the consciousness of the church at large later. Scholarship had devastating effects upon any theology that depended upon the literal credibility of all the Bible. But after biblical criticism does its utmost in stripping down the core of authentic records and sayings of Jesus, the remainder is still in Kierkegaardian terms "more than enough." Thus the contemporary unity between the most skeptical biblical scholarship and existentialism is a reasonable one.

3). Faith wants no support from external authority. Existentialism means personal decision. From Kierkegaard to Sartre the existentialists emphasize the inescapability and the glory of the freedom that takes responsibility for its own acts.

In Christian existentialism no authority can take the place of personal decision and personal trust. "No human being," writes Kierkegaard, "was ever truly an authority for another, or ever helped anyone by posing as such, or was ever able to take his client with him in truth." The one concession he makes is to grant that "one fool, when he goes astray, takes several others with him." But an external authority helps a man to truth "as little as the driver can pull the load for the horses, though he may help them by applying the lash."[6]

As Kierkegaard attacks the usefulness of the authority of the church, its officials, and the crowd, all of whom distort Christian truth better than they voice it, he sounds like an extremely rigorous Luther refighting the battle of the Reformation. But he goes further than Luther when he includes even the Bible in his biting comments:

> Fundamentally a reformation which did away with the Bible would now be just as valid as Luther's doing away with the Pope. All that about the Bible has developed a religion of learning and law, a mere distraction. . . . Christendom has long been in need of a hero who, in fear and trembling before God, had the courage to forbid people to read the Bible.

[6] Søren Kierkegaard, *Philosophical Fragments*, pp. 7, 8.

Let us collect all the New Testaments there are in existence, let us carry them out to an open place or up upon a mountain, and then, while we all kneel down, let someone address God in this fashion: Take this book back again; we men, such as we are now, are no good at dealing with a thing like this, it only makes us unhappy.[7]

These caustic remarks will lead to misunderstanding if we concentrate on them apart from Kierkegaard's own constant use of the Bible. The point is that men are capable of using even the Bible as protection against God. Absolutely nothing objective, even when enthroned to the highest authority, can do the work of personal faith.

4). Finally, doctrine is no support for faith and usually not even a healthy expression of faith. Doctrine objectifies faith and makes it a subject for discussion, thus detaching it from commitment. People are judged to be Christians because they hold sound doctrine, though they are not disciples of Christ. In New Testament faith the issue is not to hold the right concept of Christ, but to become contemporaneous with him, that is, to share his sufferings.

Kierkegaard is especially contemptuous of the professor of theology, who makes his living teaching doctrine. Christ calls men to follow him. The professor, instead of following, becomes professor of the fact that Christ called men to follow. Obviously Kierkegaard cannot entirely avoid doctrine in his own writings, and he ridicules bad doctrine. But even the best doctrine, he believes, cannot do much for faith. And it may, by shifting the central issues from obedience to discussion, interfere with faith.

In these several ways, then, Christian existentialism insists that nothing can be a substitute for genuine faith. Søren Kierkegaard derided all the customary props of faith—natural theology and rational metaphysics, history, authority, and

[7] *The Journals of Kierkegaard, 1834–1854*, trans. Alexander Dru (New York: Oxford University Press, 1938), Entries 847, 1340

doctrine—as hazards to faith. Not all Christian existentialists endorse Kierkegaard's tirades, but all have learned from him. Clearly he set in motion a major reconsideration of the meaning of Christianity and called for a thorough recasting of its most customary expressions.

Later I shall return to some of the problems existentialism raises for faith. Before that, it will be useful to look at the kaleidoscopic consequences of its impact.

III. EXISTENTIALIST PATHWAYS

Obviously there can be no unity in existentialism *per se.* Since existentialism demands free personal decision and rejects all external norms for decision, it cannot tell anyone what decision to make. Since it starts from the absurdities of experience, it cannot offer a harmony of convictions. Its impact has been more notable for power than for direction. Sometimes it resembles a rocket landing in a munitions dump, setting off explosions in uncontrollable chaos.

Kierkegaard's "leap" carried him into the arms of the God of love who had already "leaped" into existence in Christ. Nietzsche, another of the pioneer existentialists, urged an opposite leap. Since mankind has killed God, he cried, the only adequate atonement is for men to *become* gods. From the existentialist starting point men can readily move to Heidegger's declaration of the "absence of God," to Sartre's defiant atheism, to Camus's tragic humanism. Those theologians who are influenced by existentialism have been notably appreciative of *some* contemporary atheism, seeing in it an authentic protest against the idolatries of culture and religion. To decide against God, says Martin Buber, is better than to drift endlessly without making any decision. Paul Tillich, Nicholas Berdyaev, and Jacques Maritain have written with high appreciation of serious existentialist atheism, while finally confronting it with serious faith. Here is evidence of the way in which existentialist motifs run through a great variety of religious thought—atheistic, Jewish, Protestant, Eastern Orthodox, and Roman Catholic. Existentialism belongs to no one group, but has influenced many.

1. Protestant Existentialism

In the realm of theology Protestantism has the greatest native affinity with existentialism. If this sounds like the boast of a Protestant writer, I can answer that the point is made often by non-Protestants as an accusation. The implicit existentialism of Martin Luther contained most of the germs of the explicit existentialism of Kierkegaard, however much the latter aimed his polemic at Protestantism. In the wide-ranging spectrum of Protestant theologies one may find every attitude toward existentialism, but no one can doubt its power in the twentieth-century theological renaissance.

We can see its impulse in the dominant theologian of the movement, Karl Barth. In 1921 his preface to the major revision of his *Epistle to the Romans* (first published in 1918) pointed to the influence of Kierkegaard and Dostoevski. In a sentence that has become famous he wrote: ". . . if I have a system, it is limited to a recognition of what Kierkegaard called the 'infinite qualitative distinction between time and eternity' . . ."[8] Barth's writings in this period exhibit both the strenuous force and the peculiar motifs of existentialism.

As Barth became increasingly the systematic theologian, he turned his criticisms against existentialism. The clash came on several issues. Barth wanted to develop a radically biblical theology, dependent on no specific philosophy, existentialist or otherwise. Furthermore, his own Calvinism, with its emphasis on objective doctrine and the Word of God, clashed increasingly with the intensely introspective tenden-

---

8 Karl Barth, *The Epistle to the Romans*, trans. Edwyn C. Hoskyns (London: Oxford University Press, 1933), "The Preface to the Second Edition," p. 10.

cies of existentialism. More recently the thoroughgoing doctrine of incarnation in Barth has led to so strong a confidence in God's triumph over evil that the existentialist themes of struggle and despair are silenced.

Yet Barth's mature (perhaps his final) theological position, although it emphasizes "the objectivity which is indispensable to good theology," shows a critical appreciation of existentialism:

> Certainly existentialism may have reminded us once again of the elements of truth in the old school by introducing once more the thought that one cannot speak of God without speaking of man. It is to be hoped that it will not lead us back into the old error that one can speak of man without first, and very concretely, having spoken of the living God.[9]

If one asks today where Barth stands in relation to existentialism, the answer is that he is not much concerned with the question. He has developed a monumental theology, a "church dogmatics," centering more directly than any before in Jesus Christ. Whether the huge system happens to include or exclude much of existentialism is of little importance to Barth. The observer, however, can readily see how strongly existentialism has affected the Barthian pilgrimage.

Turning from Barth to Rudolf Bultmann, we find a full-fledged existentialism. Bultmann's theology, the chief European competitor to Barth's, is an attempt to express the *kerygma* (the basic proclamation) of the New Testament with frequent reference to Heidegger's philosophy. The immediate question is, Why Heidegger? If not the atheist he has often been thought to be, Heidegger is certainly no Christian. But exactly this is the fascination of Bultmann's enterprise. Instead of taking a philosopher more friendly to Christianity and the European religious tradition (for example, Jaspers), he takes the philosophy of thorough doubt

9 Karl Barth, *The Humanity of God*, trans. John N. Thomas (Richmond: John Knox Press, 1960), pp. 56–57.

where man's lostness and movement toward death get profound expression. It is precisely this situation, says Bultmann, to which the Gospel must be addressed.[10]

In a sense Bultmann is doing in contemporary culture what Kierkegaard did a century earlier when he united radical doubt with Lutheran faith. Meanwhile the intellectual situation has changed. When Kierkegaard waved aside most of the New Testament as unnecessary, he was not bluffing, but he did not actually expect the records to be invalidated. If he had been bluffing, we might now say that history has called his bluff. New Testament scholarship, as Bultmann exercises it, has questioned the historicity of the documents until little is left beyond Kierkegaard's "more than enough." Many scholars think that Bultmann, because he rejoices in the lack of objective historical evidence for Christian faith, has become far more skeptical than sound historical research demands.

One might describe Bultmann's theology as the union of maximum faith (in terms of trust and commitment) with maximum skepticism (in terms of history and traditional doctrine). This union gets eloquent expression in one of his sermons: "To refuse to believe on Jesus does not mean to reject as incredible some curious doctrines about Him, but

10 Many debates have raged about the extent of Bultmann's reliance upon Heidegger. At one point Bultmann went so far as to say: "Heidegger's existentialist analysis of the ontological structure of being would seem to be no more than a secularized, philosophical version of the New Testament view of human life." (In H. W. Bartsch, ed., *Kerygma and Myth*, London: S.P.C.K., 1953, pp. 24–25.) Later Bultmann carefully qualified this statement. He stated that Heidegger's existentialism, which was possible only because of the influence of "Paul, Augustine, Luther, and Kierkegaard," gave an accurate analysis of human existence. But, he continued, "Another question naturally concerns the *realization* of authenticity. On that matter only faith has the answer." This faith, for Bultmann, is the subject of "the existential understanding of the New Testament." ("Reply to Interpretation and Criticism," in Charles W. Kegley, *The Theology of Rudolf Bultmann* [New York: Harper & Row, 1966], pp. 259, 260.)

to refuse to allow His validity as God's challenge to the world. . . ."[11] Kierkegaard was ready in principle to brush aside the "curious doctrines"; Bultmann does so in fact. Bultmann's critics argue that he loses too much of the substance of Christian faith. His admirers hold that, by discarding the bewildering accessories, Bultmann actually locates the real substance of faith.

If Barth and Bultmann are now elder statesmen of European theology, younger men have taken up the existentialist themes and pushed them in different directions. The "post-Bultmannians," as they are sometimes called, start from a paradoxical situation. On the one hand, they recognize that Christian faith has its source in the Bible; on the other hand, they agree with Kierkegaard and Bultmann that the Bible is no objective authority validating faith. The result is that everything hinges upon *interpretation* of the Bible. The real issue is not, "What do the Scriptures say in some isolated impregnability?" but, "What do the Scriptures say to the person or community reading them in faith?"

Hence hermeneutics, the traditional term for interpretation of Scripture, has attained a new prominence and a new meaning in the work of such men as Ernst Fuchs, Gerhard Ebeling, and Heinrich Ott. In its contemporary usage, hermeneutics may be defined as "the science of reflecting on how a word or event in a past time and culture may be understood and become existentially meaningful in our present situation."[12] The process involves both historical-literary methodology and the self-understanding of the interpreter.

The post-Bultmannians find a fascination in Heidegger rather different from Bultmann's. Rudolf Bultmann draws upon Heidegger's analysis of human existence in his major

[11] Rudolf Bultmann, *This World and the Beyond*, trans. Harold Knight (New York: Charles Scribner's Sons, 1960), p. 67.

[12] Carl E. Braaten, *History and Hermeneutics* (Philadelphia: Westminster Press 1966), p. 131.

early work, *Being and Time*. The devotees of hermeneutics are attracted by the preoccupation with language in "the later Heidegger," who describes language as "the house of being" and holds that in language being is both disclosed and concealed.[13] The event, which has been so important to the Christian concept of historical revelation, becomes primarily *word-event* or *language-event*. To its practioners, this method frees the Bible from futile controversies and reinstates it in its revelatory power. To critics, the idea that Jesus is primarily a *language-event* is an inconceivable reduction of the meaning of Christian faith.[14]

When we turn to the American scene, we face immediately the powerful figure of Paul Tillich. The great originality and the great problem in Tillich's thought center in his effort to combine a strenuous existentialism with the building of the kind of theological system that Kierkegaard thought impossible. His debt to existentialism is so great that he can write, "The Existentialist revolt is the decisive event, theoretical and practical, of the last one hundred years."[15] That, in the century that included Marx and Stalin, Hitler, Einstein, and the development of nuclear warfare, is a strong statement. Yet Tillich, replying to Father Gustave Weigel, can say: "With respect to my ontological thought generally,

[13] See the discussion of Heidegger by Stanley Romaine Hopper, Ch. III, Part IX, below.

[14] The discussions of the European post-Bultmannians, in interaction with American theologians and biblical scholars, are conveniently available in three books edited by James M. Robinson and John B. Cobb: *The Later Heidegger and Theology, The New Hermeneutic*, and *Theology as History* (New York: Harper & Row, 1963, 1964, and 1967). Cf. also the papers of the Third Consultation on Hermeneutics convened at Drew University in April, 1966, published in *Interpretation: The Poetry of Meaning*, ed. Stanley Romaine Hopper and David L. Miller (New York: Harcourt, Brace, and World, Inc., 1967).

[15] Paul Tillich, "The Person in a Technical Society," in *Christian Faith and Social Action*, ed. John A. Hutchison (New York: Charles Scribner's Sons, 1953), p. 145.

I want to state that it is much less influenced by existentialism than by Aristotle and Schelling. It is my doctrine concerning man in which the influence of existentialism is
important."[16] The reference to Schelling is not surprising,
since Tillich has long regarded him as an ancestor of existentialism.[17] But the mention of Aristotle poses a different
set of problems.

To unite an existential and biblical doctrine of man
with classical ontology is a bold endeavor and, when under-
taken by a brilliant mind like Tillich's, a fertile one. If it
succeeds, it is an achievement for the centuries. Certainly
Tillich made a valiant effort. In *The Courage to Be*, where
he often comes close to Heidegger, and in *The Dynamics of
Faith*, where he defines faith existentially as ultimate concern, he expresses his existentialism. In his *Systematic Theology* he is the speculative system-builder. The remarkable
thing is the force of the existentialist thrust in the system and
the expression of the system in the shorter, more existentialist
writings.

Reinhold Niebuhr, Tillich's long-time friend and col-
league, is both more and less existentialist than Tillich.
Throughout much of his career Niebuhr has concentrated on
social ethics and political philosophy. He has studied the
nature of politics and history, including the structures of
social organization in which men act. Social philosophy, especially in its structural aspects, is the area in which existentialism with its inward preoccupation has contributed least.
Hence Niebuhr's thought, concerned with the exercise of
political power and with international relations, has moved
in areas distant from the introspective brooding that existentialists sometimes cultivate.

[16] Gustave Weigel, S.J., "The Theological Significance of Paul Tillich,"
Gregorianum, Vol. XXXVII, 1 (1956), p. 54.

[17] See Paul Tillich, "Existential Philosophy," *Journal of the History of
Ideas*, January, 1944, pp. 44ff. The same essay, it should be noted, points out
the kinship between Aristotle and Heidegger.

Niebuhr's doctrine of man started as a doctrine of political man. But Kierkegaard helped him to illuminate the relation between the political impulse to build empires or enslave races and the inner anxieties of the self. Martin Buber's conception of the self in its I-Thou relations contributed to his understanding of personality. Thus Niebuhr united personal-existentialist with social-political insights into man.

The existentialist protest against rational systems is congenial to Niebuhr's political and theological thinking. The system-buiders, he maintains, "know too much." Niebuhr's theology rigorously excludes every doctrinal element that lacks experimental reference. He is the empiricist rather than the rationalist, if empiricism may be taken to refer to the heights and depths of experience as well as to sensory perception. Existentialist man cannot rise out of existence to survey the world. In his finitude, anxiety, and guilt he lives his experience and reasons about it. And by the grace of God he may live in faith.

Some younger Protestant thinkers have developed a more radical existentialism than that of Tillich or Niebuhr. They are engaged in intensive conversations about hermeneutics, both among themselves and with the post-Bultmannians in Europe. Among them are James M. Robinson and the late Carl Michalson, whose death in an air crash at the age of fifty ended prematurely the career of a sensitive and imaginative thinker. At present it is too early to tell whether they are riding the crest of a wave that will soon collapse or are the forward edge of a flood that will dominate the future.

2. Catholic Traditions

Catholic thought in all its varieties must immediately contest some of the elements of existentialism that are most akin to Protestantism. To many a thinker in the Catholic traditions, Eastern or Western, existentialism is the final fruit of Luther's worst heresies. Yet in the great theological stirring of the twentieth century Eastern Orthodox and Roman Catholic theologians have learned from Kierkegaard and his heirs.

All the Catholic systems traditionally put great emphasis on the church with its cult, hierarchy, visible apostolic succession, definitions of dogma, sacred tradition, and institutions. Such religion cannot readily absorb the existentialist rejection of all external, objective supports to faith. Roman Catholicism has two additional features that are targets for existentialist attack: an official natural theology, formulated in the Thomist arguments for the existence of God, and an infallible authority vested in the Pope.

Nevertheless existentialism has assaulted these barriers and exercised some theological influence. The Eastern Orthodox world, with its loyalty to the dogmas of the ancient councils, might seem immune to any revolutionary change. But wherever the turbulent spirit of Dostoevski sways men, the existentialist motifs gain a hearing. Dostoevski's heroes—tormented by anxieties, torn between nihilistic doubt and passionate faith, thirsting for freedom—are genuine existentialists. Nicholas Berdyaev, the Russian who spent much of his career in exile in Paris, was a scholar of Dostoevski, a boldly imaginative theologian, and a man who in writing and in act celebrated the freedom of the human spirit. Asked about existentialism, he once replied: "Existentialism?—But I *am* existentialism!"[18]

In the Church of Rome existentialism is checked by Thomist theology and the principle of authority. But the Augustinian spirit, partly absorbed in and partly contesting with Thomism, exerts a strong thrust toward existentialism. I have already noted the work of Pascal, whose *Pensées* reflect his lostness in the silence of infinite spaces, the impossibility

[18] Reported by Roger Troisfontaines, S.J., *Existentialism and Christian Thought* (Westminster: Dacre Press, 1949), p. 1.

of reasoning his way to God, and the glory and misery of man. Pascal was a heretic, and any Roman Catholic existentialist must skirt the borders of orthodoxy. But in some cases the wildness of the existentialist spirit, made more temperate by orthodox discipline, leads to a peculiarly persuasive theology.

In the United States official Catholicism has until recently attacked or ignored existentialism. But some lay writers have taken a different direction. Erich Frank's profound works[19] stand in the Augustinian tradition and include a Kierkegaardian thrust. Jacques Maritain has to do some playing with words to make his claim that St. Thomas is the truest existentialist, but he does show considerable appreciation of Kierkegaardian motifs.[20] Maritain shows a very real existentialism of his own in the brilliant essay, "The Meaning of Contemporary Atheism,[21] where he breaks through the conventional debates of our time to a penetrating interpretation of the modern spiritual struggle.

European Catholicism shows many varieties of existentialist expression. Enrico Castelli of Rome, appealing to the tradition of Bonaventure, assaults Heidegger but insists that revelation is the presupposition (rather than the completion) of medieval philosophy.[22] Roger Troisfontaines, the Belgian Jesuit, holds that Christianity combines the objective and the subjective, but has been expressed in the West chiefly within an objective philosophy. Hence, "Existentialism gives scholasticism the chance of rejuvenation by taking a dose of 'subjectivity.' "[23]

[19] See especially *Philosophical Understanding and Religious Truth* (New York: Oxford University Press, 1945).

[20] Jacques Maritain, *Existence and the Existent* (New York: Pantheon Books, 1948).

[21] In Jacques Maritain, *The Range of Reason* (New York: Charles Scribner's Sons, 1952).

[22] Enrico Castelli, *Existentialisme Théologique* (Paris: Hermann & Cie., 1948).

[23] Roger Troisfontaines, S.J., *Existentialism and Christian Thought*, p. 37.

In France existentialism has made its greatest Roman Catholic penetration. The layman, Gabriel Marcel, has expressed it in dramas and philosophical writings. A large group of Frenchmen, including priests and laymen, have shown a variety of existentialist and personalist strains in their writing. Some of them, notably Emmanuel Mounier, have reached American audiences through the distinguished journal *Cross Currents*.

Inevitably some of these writings have strained the bounds of orthodoxy and aroused official hostility. In the Encyclical *Humani Generis*, 1950, Pope Pius XII declared false any existentialism which "concerns itself only with the existence of individual things and neglects all consideration of their immutable essences." He reasserted the validity of church dogma, of natural theology, and of "the mind's ability to attain certain and unchangeable truth." Among the targets of his attack were the existentialist tendency to mythological and paradoxical thinking. And he rejected "existentialism, whether atheistic or simply the type that denies the validity of the reason in the field of metaphysics."[24]

The encyclical appeared to many to be a condemnation of some of the most creative Roman Catholic thinking. Such scholars as Jean Daniélou, Henri de Lubac, Georges Yves Congar, and Karl Rahner came under its cloud. They continued their work, but their influence was cramped. However Vatican Council II with its opening of the windows (to use Pope John XXIII's phrase) has brought increased prominence to some of these men and has enlarged the freedom that the existentialist impulse craves. Current Catholic theology makes obsolete all the clichés of its critics.

3. Conflicting Themes in Judaism

It might seem unnecessary to justify existentialism among the people who wrote the Psalms, Job, and the book

---

[24] Pope Pius XII, *Humani Generis*, official English translation, *New York Times*, August 22, 1950, p. 16.

of the prophet Jeremiah. Existentialism would seem to be even more native to the Jewish mind than to the Christian, where the Hebrew confrontation with life mingles with the Greek ambition for building rational metaphysical systems.

But Judaism, as the religion of a people, has a strong sense of community that modifies, often in healthy ways, existentialist individualism. Furthermore Judaism has always been the religion of the law and the prophets. Wherever the law—especially the ceremonial law—attains great importance, it conflicts with the existentialist attack upon the validity of external supports for faith.

Hence traditional Judaism is not entirely congenial to existentialism. Modern Judaism adds one more source of opposition insofar as it draws much of its ethic from the Enlightenment. It is easy to see why Judaism, after suffering bitter persecution from Christians, should rejoice in the tolerance and freedom of eighteenth-century rationalism. Reform Judaism, in particular, has grasped the Enlightenment ethic to its heart. Reading the prophets, it finds the message of justice and universalism—which is clearly of fundamental importance. It neglects the themes that the existentialists are likely to treasure most: the awareness of the insecurity of all things human, the loneliness of the prophet alienated from the people he loves, the tremors of the spirit searching out its own anxieties and sins, the radical trust in and communion with God.

Marvin Fox, an able philosopher and Orthodox Jew, has compared the rabbinic treatment with Kierkegaard's use of the story of Abraham's offering of Isaac. He concludes that Kierkegaard's "doctrines are, on the whole, antithetical to traditional Jewish beliefs."[25] Despite considerable appreciation of Kierkegaard, Fox sees in him an opposition to "the usual Jewish optimism," to the Jewish effort to make faith as

25 Marvin Fox, "Kierkegaard and Rabbinic Judaism," *Judaism*, Vol. II (1953), p. 160. Fox discusses other recent Jewish treatments of the same subject.

rational as possible, to the readiness to call even God to account by standards of justice, to the vivid Jewish awareness of community. Several of these comments raise cogent issues, which anyone must take seriously. At the moment I simply point them out as typical of much of the Jewish criticism of existentialism.

Nevertheless some of the great pioneers of modern existentialism have come from the Jewish community. Among the foremost is surely Franz Kafka, whose novels have a large place in any listing of the existentialist scriptures. *The Trial* and *The Castle* express the alienation, the ambiguity and absurdity, the union of despair with intimations of grace that are so characteristic of existentialism.

Among Jewish theologians two friends and colleagues, Franz Rosenzweig and Martin Buber, led the existentialist revolution in central Europe after the first World War. Rosenzweig's thought had unmistakable affinities with Kierkegaard and Nietzsche, but he was profoundly Jewish and concentrated much of his writing on the mystery of Israel.[26] His tragic career—eight years of progressive paralysis brought him to death at the age of forty-three in 1929—made of him a legend that reinforced the existentialist power of his works.

Martin Buber collaborated with Rosenzweig in a new German translation of the Bible. In his long career Buber's influence has extended over Europe, America, and Israel. A scholar of the Bible, philosophy, psychology, and the social sciences, Buber has offered fresh and illuminating insights to Christian theology, even though Christians in their pride are often unready to learn from Jews. His short but great work, *I and Thou*, has furnished the vocabulary and the ideas for much contemporary theological discussion. As the Postscript to the second edition of that book shows, Buber has moved

[26] A substantial selection from Rosenzweig's writings is available in English in *Franz Rosenzweig: His Life and Thought*, presented by Nahum N. Glatzer (New York: Schocken Books, revised ed., 1961).

steadily from his early mysticism to an increasingly biblical and existentialist sense of life as decision, freedom, and personal encounter.[27]

Perhaps Buber's two most important contributions to theology are his confrontation of faith with doubt and his powerful perception of the meaning of human community. Dealing with the first issue, he has acknowledged the genius of Nietzsche, acclaiming the rebellious vitality of his thought and opposing it with faith. In *The Eclipse of God* and other works he shows the meaning of faith in an era of profound doubt. On the second issue he has adopted the inner penetration of Kierkegaard and modified it with his strong sense of personal relations. Confronting the Kierkegaardian question, "Who am I?" Buber shows that every genuine *I* is a participant in *I-Thou* relations, that indeed there can be no *I* except as there is *Thou*. *Between Man and Man* combines the appreciation of selfhood with the attack upon individualism as brilliantly as anything in contemporary literature.

Following Rosenzweig and Buber, Judaism has seen some original and provocative second-generation thinkers who offer existentialist versions of faith. Abraham Joshua Heschel, author of *God in Search of Man*, blends biblical, mystical, and existentialist insights in a sensitive theology. Will Herberg in *Judaism and Modern Man* and in numerous shorter writings develops an existentialist version of Judaism in conversation with contemporary philosophy, sociology, and culture. Although both of these thinkers stand on the edge of Judaism's main stream, they have strong influence both within and outside Judaism.

IV. SOME BURNING ISSUES

Thus far I have described the impact of existentialism as a kindling, perhaps explosive force in the theological revo-

27 Martin Buber, *I and Thou* (New York: Charles Scribner's Sons, second ed., 1958).

lution of our era. Occasionally along the way I have indicated difficult issues that it raises. The time has come to examine some of these issues.

1. *Truth and Commitment*

Existentialism calls for decision—for an act of radical freedom issuing in resolute involvement and commitment. Since it tells every person that his decision must be his own, it cannot prescribe decisions for anyone. It may go so far as to reject all norms of decision and to deny importance to the content of the decision. In Kierkegaard's vocabulary, for example, *truth* attaches more to the deciding person than to the objective choice that he makes.

> If one who lives in the midst of Christendom goes up to the house of God, the house of the true God, with the true conception of God in his knowledge, and prays, but prays in a false spirit; and one who lives in an idolatrous community prays with the entire passion of the infinite, although his eyes rest upon the image of an idol: where is there most truth? The one prays in truth to God though he worships an idol; the other prays falsely to the true God, and hence worships in fact an idol.[28]

Kierkegaard assumes, we should note, that there is a true God and a true conception of God, but he attaches the more important truth to the manner of worship. His example is persuasive because it assumes an innocent idolater as compared with a hypocritical or indecisive Christian. But existentialist reasoning might use other examples, declaring a Hitler to live in greater truth than a moderately decent person who lacked the Nazi intensity of decision.

As usual, however, Kierkegaard has anticipated the criticism. "What objections can be brought against this man that he himself has not already more accurately stated?" asks Denis de Rougemont.[29] Almost as though he had foreseen the

---

[28] Søren Kierkegaard, *Concluding Unscientific Postscript*, pp. 179–180.
[29] *Love in the Western World* (New York: Pantheon Books, revised ed., 1956), p. 130.

writings of Nietzsche, Kierkegaard attacked the "devilish" wisdom that sometimes arises in existentialism:

> It perceives that all depends upon the will and so it proclaims loudly, "Unless it wills one thing, a man's life is sure to become one of wretched mediocrity, of pitiful misery. He must will one thing regardless of whether it be good or bad. He must will one thing, for therein lies a man's greatness." Yet it is not difficult to see through his powerful error. . . . Salvation, therefore, lies only in the purity with which a man wills the Good.[30]

This latter confession, it may be argued, stems less from Kierkegaard's existentialism as such than from his Christian faith. Critics have argued that, just as Nietzschian existentialism is a kind of super-Prometheanism, so Kierkegaardian existentialism is a super-Pelagianism. In some ways the charge is clearly mistaken: the contrast between the simple Pelagian moral psychology and the sophisticated Kierkegaardian exploration of selfhood is immense. But if ancient Pelagianism assumed that man could live virtuously by an act of will, existentialism sometimes suggests that he can will the truth or even will God into reality. "God is a subject, and therefore exists only for subjectivity in inwardness," writes Kierkegaard.[31] Nietzsche, we have seen, would have men become gods. Sartre calls on men, since God is dead, to create their own values. Yet Kierkegaard, if not Nietzsche and Sartre, knows better. "Faith is not an act of will,"[32] but a work of God's grace.

Like American pragmatism, existentialism sometimes blurs the difference between the truth that can be *produced* by commitment and the truth that can be *known* only in commitment. William James argued that "faith in a fact can help create the fact"—a proposition that may be convincing for winning a football game or a woman's love, possibly for

---

30 Søren Kierkegaard, *Purity of Heart Is to Will One Thing,* trans. Douglas Steere (New York: Harper & Row, 1938), pp. 35–36.

31 *Concluding Unscientific Postscript,* p. 178.

32 *Philosophical Fragments,* p. 50.

entering into a relationship with God, but not for creating the reality of God. He also defended faith as the necessary condition for "acknowledging certain kinds of truth" that are really true—a reasoning that can make sense in regard to God.[33] Voluntaristic philosophies sometimes obscure the difference between these two kinds of faith and thus assign to the will an impossible role in determining truth.

In actual fact no existentialist can ignore completely the content of truth. Kierkegaard, despite all his polemics against doctrine and in favor of discipleship, often came around to the statement of Christian doctrine—formulating it in ways that may have been unnecessarily paradoxical and irrational.

The issue becomes even more obvious in respect to ethics. The emphasis on will in contrast to content means that existentialists find themselves on every side of every struggle, accusing their opponents of bad faith. The resulting chaos becomes the urgent occasion for recognition of norms. Some of the most existentially inclined theologians have criticized the excessive voluntarism in contemporary ethics. Thus Paul Tillich has written of "the voluntaristic distortion of faith."[34] Reinhold Niebuhr, while often maintaining that human nature has "a freedom beyond structure," also argues against Sartre that it has a "basic structure."[35] Will Herberg, who once saw no good in ethical theories of natural law, has come to ask for a "serious rethinking of the natural law tradition."[36]

2. Existentialism and Logical Empiricism

Related to the issue of commitment and truth is the curious kinship between existentialism and logical empiri-

[33] See William James, "The Will to Believe," many editions, sections IX, X.

[34] *The Dynamics of Faith* (New York: Harper & Row, 1957), pp. 35–38.

[35] *The Self and the Dramas of History* (New York: Charles Scribner's Sons, 1955), pp. 65–68.

[36] "Historicism as Touchstone," in the series, "How My Mind Has Changed," *The Christian Century*, Vol. LXXVII (1960), pp. 311–313.

cism. In the early years of both movements the opposition between them seemed complete. Existentialism with its romantic impulses and its urge to commitment had nothing to do with logical empiricism (then called positivism) with its antiseptic scientific ambition. Few noticed in those days how much of traditional nominalism entered into both movements.

Today the two have often come into congenial union. If logical empiricism excludes from knowledge all metaphysics and normative ethics, it does not eliminate the need for men to act. The new breed of philosopher no less than his predecessors must decide whether to marry, pay his taxes, and heed the draft call. His decisions, unsupported by traditional philosophical methods, become remarkably like the existentialist's act of decision.

Many contemporary theologians have drawn together elements of existentialism and logical empiricism. Doing this to a moderate degree Reinhold Niebuhr has appropriated much of the empirical protest against metaphysics. In a far more radical way Willem Zuurdeeg accepted the logical positivist's case against metaphysics, then made his existentialist decision in terms of a Barthian type of faith.[37] Many of the younger theologians of this country have worked on various types of the synthesis. No one has succeeded, however, in stating a doctrine of God (probably not even a doctrine of man) without metaphysical implications. If a thinker must get into metaphysics, he had better admit the fact.

One aspect of this tendency, which I have already noted in Part I of this essay, is the removal of all philosophical support for belief. Most of life's normal decisions can be explained reasonably in terms of more fundamental decisions. But finally the process drives the explainer to a rock-bottom decision, which rests on nothing outside itself. Such, say the existentialists, is the religious decision. One can confess it

[37] *An Analytical Philosophy of Religion* (Nashville: Abingdon Press, 1958).

and proclaim it, but not defend it. If one confesses that Christ has saved him from his sins, says Kierkegaard, all argument is useless:

> There the only conceivable objection would be: but you might possibly have been saved in a different way. To that he cannot answer. It is as though one were to say to someone in love, yes, but you might have fallen in love with another girl: to which he would have to answer: there is no answer to that, for I only know that she is my love. The moment a lover can answer that objection he is *eo ipso* not in love. If a believer can answer that objection he is *eo ipso* not a believer.[38]

Kierkegaard is right in the sense that there is no argument with experience. What he neglects in this comment is the implicit claim of religious confession to a wider than strictly personal truth, usually to a universal truth. When a Christian testifies to Christ, he says by implication that what Christ has done for him, he will do for others who trust him. When a man testifies to what his wife has done for him, he is *not* saying that she will do the same for others. It is the universal claim inherent in religious confession that leads to the apologetic enterprise.

Actually Kierkegaard and many other existentialists are skilled apologists—not in the sense of arguing for faith on grounds other than faith, but in the sense of showing the significance of faith for human anxiety, guilt, and a wide range of experiences. Whenever they claim any truth for faith beyond the sheer assertion, "I will" or "I feel," they break out of the alliance with the most rigid logical empiricisms.

3. Individualism and Community

The exaltation of personal decision may lead to an individualism so intense as to be unrealistic in a world where human nature is always the nature of man in community. Existentialism, in its cogent protest against a world that re-

[38] *The Journals of Kierkegaard, 1834–1854,* Entry 922.

duces men to anonymous bits of a mass, has sometimes fallen into this extreme individualism.

Kierkegaard, describing the "knight of faith," says that this pilgrim knows well the joys of companionship and of belonging to "the universal."

> But he knows also that higher than this there winds a solitary path, narrow and steep; he knows that it is terrible to be born outside the universal, to walk without meeting a single traveller. . . . [The knight of faith] in the solitude of the universe never hears any human voice but walks alone with his dreadful responsibility.[39]

Again Kierkegaard corrects himself when he comes to write of *The Works of Love.*[40] For love inevitably recognizes and creates community. Even here, however, H. Richard Niebuhr may have been right when he wrote that Kierkegaard "beautifully analyzes the character of true Christian love, but is more concerned with the virtue than with the beings to be loved."[41] This straining individualism persists in much of contemporary existentialism, although Martin Buber has corrected it with his strong sense of personal relations, as have many of the Catholic existentialists with their esteem for community.

It might seem that its strong personalism and individualism make impossible any major existentialist contribution to a contemporary "social gospel." Yet it may be that in this era, when persons need defense against the kindnesses as well as the cruelties of the economic and social order, the most important criticism of society comes from existentialist sources. Thus William Barrett pays tribute to Kierkegaard's "brilliantly prophetic" essay, *The Present Age*:

[39] *Fear and Trembling,* trans. Walter Lowrie (Garden City: Doubleday Anchor Books, 1954), pp. 86, 90.

[40] Princeton: Princeton University Press, 1946.

[41] H. Richard Niebuhr, *Christ and Culture* (New York: Harper & Row, 1951), p. 180.

So well has Kierkegaard's prophecy held up in fact that even contemporary efforts at journalistic sociology, like Riesman's *The Lonely Crowd* or Whyte's *The Organization Man*, are still repeating and documenting his insights.[42]

Kierkegaard's theology alone can say little about economic and racial justice or international affairs. But it makes a devastating rejection of the amalgam of religion with nationalism and social status that has made the church so ineffective in meeting its social responsibilities. When Kierkegaardian insight is joined to an awareness of the importance of social structures, as in a thinker like Reinhold Niebuhr, the result is a penetrating social ethic.

4. *Theology, History, and Nature*

Existentialism, I have argued, is the rebel offspring of biblical faith, which concentrates on historical existence, in its awareness of both the self and the activity of God. Yet many of the existentialists are so unconcerned with "objective history" that they lose the biblical sense of God's lordship over the history of nations and peoples. From all biblical history Kierkegaard needs only the one brief fragment that is "more than enough." Bultmann accepts God's historical activity only in the sense that "God is a personal being acting on persons." Therefore he rejects all the "political and juridical conceptions" in Scripture "unless they are understood purely as symbols."[43] Bultmann, I think, defends himself successfully against the frequent attack that he reduces the Christian faith to psychologism, but he does not retain much of history.

In fact, the very word "history" undergoes a subtle transmutation in the existentialist writings. It ceases to mean what the workaday historian or the average newspaper reader

---

[42] *Irrational Man*, p. 154.

[43] Rudolf Bultmann, *Jesus Christ and Mythology* (New York: Charles Scribner's Sons, 1958), p. 70.

means by history. Bultmann's theology of history almost reduces history to the meaning of the historicity (the concrete particularity in time) of the individual.[44] Starting from the irrefutable fact that biblical history is never purely external, objective history, he moves to an almost total emphasis on internal history, akin to R. G. Collingwood's philosophical idealism.[45] Karl Löwith's brilliant study all but consigns world history to the ash heap of meaninglessness.[45] Carl Michalson, after defining history in several ways, makes a sensitive analysis of the truly significant history, which is so etherealized as to have little relation to the economic-political history that most of us studied in school.[47] One must ask whether existentialism is repeating the ancient Marcionite heresy of separating the New Testament from the Old Testament, which after all said a lot about imperial dynasties, wars, and the quest for economic goods.

We must readily acknowledge that contemporary theologians do not understand history in Old Testament terms. That is, they do not think that God does everything attributed to Him in the Bible—at least not in the ways often attributed to Him there. The existentialists challenge theology to think through its assumptions with rigor and honesty.

Dietrich Bonhoeffer's powerful call for a "Christian worldliness," issued from a Nazi prison,[48] has been to many Christians a destructive blow to existentialism. Bonhoeffer, criticizing the excessive interiorization of history that he found in Bultmann and the existentialists, acclaimed Christ as Lord of the world, not merely the rescuer of men from

[44] *The Presence of Eternity: History and Eschatology* (New York: Harper & Row, 1957).

[45] *The Idea of History* (London: Oxford University Press, The Clarendon Press, 1946).

[46] *Meaning in History* (Chicago: University of Chicago Press, 1949).

[47] *The Hinge of History* (New York: Charles Scribners' Sons, 1959).

[48] Dietrich Bonhoeffer, *Letters and Papers from Prison* (New York: Macmillan Paperbacks, 1962).

anxiety. Harvey Cox, taking up Bonhoeffer's theme, sees existentialism as "the last child of a cultural epoch, born in its mother's senility," totally unable to cope with the contemporary secular world.[49] But the attack may overlook some of the resources of existentialism. Carl Michalson, perhaps the most radically existentialist of American theologians, entitled his final, posthumously published book, *Worldly Theology* and found the secularizing impulses of Bonhoeffer thoroughly congenial with his own existentialist sense that theology finds reality only in historical commitment.[50]

A somewhat comparable problem arises with regard to nature. Mario Praz[51] has shown how the underside of the romantic movement saw a hypnotic fascination in misery, horror, and death, in sin and Satan, in morbid sexual pathology and cruelty. Anyone reading Praz is bound to see the continuation of these themes in much of the existentialist writing, especially fiction and drama, of our time. Here is the recurrence of the ancient Manichean heresy, which declared the created world to be evil.

Strains of this heresy have sifted into theological existentialism, though less pervasively than in atheistic philosophies. Kierkegaard himself is not free from this tendency. He could say that "love of God is hatred of the world."[52] "Christianity in the New Testament consists in loving God, in hatred to man, in hatred of oneself, and thereby of other men, hating father, mother, one's own child, wife, etc., the strongest expression for the most agonizing isolation."[53] Obviously the reference is primarily to the cultural "world,"

[49] Harvey Cox, *The Secular City* (New York: The Macmillan Co., 1965), p. 252.

[50] Carl Michalson, *Worldly Theology: The Hermeneutical Focus of an Historical Faith* (New York: Charles Scribner's Sons, 1967).

[51] *The Romantic Agony* (New York: Meridian Books, 1956).

[52] *Training in Christianity*, p. 218.

[53] *Attack upon "Christendom"*, trans. Walter Lowrie (Princeton University Press, 1944), p. 163.

but it spills over into the total world. Obviously, too, Kierkegaard can find texts of Scripture to back up his violent statements. What he forgets at times are other texts. "For God so
loved the world that he gave his only Son . . ." (John 3:16).

Yet, as so often, Kierkegaard is his own best critic. He
learned to write of his own suffering (at the hands of nature
and of culture) without a trace of Manicheism or world
hatred:

> The birds on the branches, the lilies in the field, the deer in
> the forest, the fish in the sea, countless hosts of happy men exul-
> tantly proclaim: God is love. But beneath all these sopranos, sup-
> porting them as it were, like the bass part, is audible the *de
> profundis* which issues from those who are sacrificed: God is
> love.[54]

V. CONCLUSION

If existentialism is a prodigal son of biblical theology,
the father will be both generous and wise to seek his son and
welcome him home. The household will not be more placid
when the son returns, but it will be more live and more
complete.

Existentialism is not biblical faith. It is not a substitute
for biblical faith. But the only answer to existentialism is an
existential faith. That means a faith that incorporates some
of the rebellion that authentic faith has always wrought. It
means a faith that includes those original existential elements
that, when suppressed, break forth in existentialism.

54 *The Journals of Kierkegaard, 1834–1854,* Entry 1260.

Three

LITERATURE

The Author in Search
of His Anecdote

STANLEY ROMAINE HOPPER

A triangle, according to Wittgenstein, may be standing up in
one picture, hanging in another, and something that has
fallen over in a third. The observation in itself is commonplace, and the reader is under no obligation to feel astonished
at it; but it is not as benign as it first appears, and it will
help us in a preliminary way to dispose the complex elements of "existentialist" literature in a useful, if somewhat
arbitrary, way.

In the house of existentialism today there are many
legitimate residents, whether native or naturalized; but there
are also interlopers and aliens of questionable lineage and
antecedents. "Existentialism has never existed!" exclaimed
Jean Cau, referring to the faddist fringe and the Parisienne
myth of cafe eccentrics. "It is an invention of the newspa-

pers." But with these we are not concerned. We distinguish rather in the works of the authentic existentialists a certain *triangulation* of themes (or postulations, or controlling metaphors) which the several authors hold in common, but which are postured differently. In Heidegger's picture of the human situation the triangle of postulates is presented "standing up," based upon a fundamental ontology; Kierkegaard's, on the other hand, appears to be hanging from the apex—from the Paradox, the point where "the Eternal enters into time"; whereas Sartre's somewhat somber surfaces lie sprawled in the ungainly prolapse of being into nothingness brought about by the attempt to "draw all the consequences of a coherent atheistic position."[1] Other existentialists posture the triangle still differently: any one of the three sides of the triangle may be asserted to be its proper base, any one of the three angles may be held as the apex, or the triangle itself may be seen "as a wedge, as an arrow . . ., as half a parallelogram" (Wittgenstein), or as a buttock on a cubist nude by Picasso or Braque, or (by a Thomist who will insist that "essences" precede existences) as an analogue of the Trinity. There are other possibilities. (A triangle, however postured, would have the same center; but if the existentialist triangles are whirled fast enough, will they therefore look the same?)

So far as the literature of existentialism is concerned it is important to note three things: first, that the familiar frameworks, backgrounds, settings, conventions, models for thought, etc., customarily provided by the classical tradition (including "Christendom" in its intellectualistic and substantialistic forms) have dropped away or have shattered under the percussions of change that have overtaken the Western consciousness; second, that as a result the theses of

1 Jean-Paul Sartre, *Existentialism* ("L'Existentialisme est un humanisme"), trans. Bernard Frechtman (New York: Philosophical Library, 1947), pp. 60–61.

the existentialist writers rotate centripetally about the ego in search of itself (its Self); third, that these factors make the problem of communication paramount for the literary artist.

I. THE EXISTENTIAL THEMES IN LITERATURE

The first problem—the dropping away of the frameworks and world pictures—has been put summarily by Nietzsche in his declaration that "God is dead!" The culture complex of Christendom has shattered. The symbol system elaborated under its purview no longer elicits an acknowledging response. By its signs we are no longer healed or integrated. Alienation, estrangement, isolation, fragmentation result. We become "waylost, wanderers" (MacLeish).

The spirit of Zarathustra presides over these Nietzschean reflections; but Kierkegaard's "Attack on Christendom," together with his polemic against all dogmatic fixations in favor of the faith of "inwardness," is fully as radical. Camus's "rebel" bears witness to a similar rejection of historical patterns. Ortega y Gasset put it succinctly: ". . . the European crisis, which is the world crisis, may be diagnosed as a crisis of all classicism. We feel that the traditional ways are useless to solve our problems."[2]

The radical nature of all this is indicated by Camus when he notes that we are now deprived of the mediatorial offices of the conventional institutions, and since through them we have become exiled from the orders of nature as given, "we are once again in the world of the Old Testament, crushed between a cruel Pharaoh and an implacable heaven."[3]

[2] "In Search of Goethe from Within," *The Dehumanization of Art and Other Writings on Art and Culture* (Garden City: Doubleday Anchor Book, 1956), p. 125.

[3] Albert Camus, *The Rebel, An Essay on Man in Revolt* (New York: Vintage Books, 1956), p. 300.

This is a dramatic way of putting it; but it does not go far enough. The comparison petitions an order not ours. Job—God-forsaken and desolate—is nearer to us:

> Has not man a hard service upon earth,
>   and are not his days like the days of a hireling?
> Like a slave who longs for the shadow,
>
>   .   .   .   .   .
>
> so am I allotted months of emptiness,
>   and nights of misery. . . .
>
> Job 7: 1-3

Job—in his radical rebellion against the conventional patterns of his day (including the official God-pattern)—is in fact the prototype of Camus's rebel, who, in times such as ours, must protest absolutely, in order that renewal may come:

> We are at that extremity now. At the end of this tunnel of darkness, however, there is inevitably a light, which we already divine and for which we have only to fight to ensure its coming. All of us, among the ruins, are preparing a renaissance beyond the limits of nihilism. But few of us know it.[4]

The one thing that is unimpeachable about Camus is the determined sincerity of his work and the pervasive candor of his will not to be taken in by the manifold shams of the epoch into which he was "thrown" and within which he bore an open witness to life and the world as he saw it. William Faulkner spoke well, when, in his congratulatory message to Camus on the occasion of the latter's receiving the Nobel Prize, he wrote: "On salue l'âme qui constamment se cherche et s'interroge" ("We salute the soul which constantly searches for and interrogates itself"). For this is clearly what happens when, with the loss of the sustaining frameworks and symbols, the self is thrown desperately back upon itself and is forced like Job to find a foothold within its own inner declivities.

4 *Ibid.*, p. 305.

This is the second theme recurrent in existentialist literature: viz., the rotation of the existentialist themes (turning in
toward the center) about the ego in search of itself. We see
man pressed against the "limit situations" of his humanhood
—death, suffering, pain, "shipwreck," "struggle," "nausea," the
"absurd," the "horizon," the "abyss," etc. In the "shock" of
extreme situations I am thrust up against the existential
antinomies of the human predicament. I must reach decision
concerning myself. Even *this* language remains formal and
abstract until I have myself assumed its meaning in the
moment of the absolute choice of myself. " 'S death," exclaimed Kierkegaard in his *Journals*, "I can abstract from
everything but *not from myself!*"—and with that cry out of
his inner distress extentialism was born.

This is the point, of course, from which our scrutiny of
the existentialist literature should begin. There is, however,
a third side of the "triangulation" of themes which now appears. This is the problem of communication. More precisely,
it is the problem of communicating in a manner or mode
consistent with the philosophical stance outlined in steps
one and two above. Kierkegaard put it sharply, as usual, by
indicating that it was once considered impossible to paint
Mars in the armor that made him invisible; but the propo-
nents of objective writing (the classicists and works compliant
with the "system") appear to manage this quite easily. The
literary work is "objective," it is about someone else, it is
conducted in the past, its form is outside the reader and ob-
servable, and it culminates in a satisfactory *result*. In such
literature there "are no secrets." Only thinking which is
"doubly reflected" (which involves or returns upon the
thinker who is thinking) has such secrets. "Wherever the subjective is of importance in knowledge, and where appropriation thus constitutes the crux of the matter, the process of
communication is *a work of art*, and doubly reflected."[5] What

---

[5] *Concluding Unscientific Postscript*, trans. Walter Lowrie (Princeton:
Princeton University Press, 1941), p. 73; italics added.

the reader perceives in the work of art as the author's reflection is reflected back upon himself as involved in the predicament. The problem of communication—the problem of bringing the double reflection about—is the third side of the triangle; and this recognition is common to existentialist literature generally.

At this point, however, the practitioners of the existentialist "art of communication" divide. The division is not so much *between* the existentialist writers as it is *within* the complex of existentialist claims. All recognize in the problem of communication three factors: (1) the factor or phase of existential analysis, (2) the aspect of maieutic artistry whereby the reader is led into some sort of self-confrontation, and (3) the hoped for "reversal" (into "commitment," "engagement," "involvement," "witness," "apostleship," "guardianship" or "shepherdship of being," "festivity," or "celebration").

Here also is a triangle of possibilities which may be differently positioned while the same three emphases are retained. "Lucidity," so greatly prized by the French existentialists, may be refracted from many angles. Ionesco's *Rhinoceros* and Kafka's *Metamorphosis* have something in common, but the theme of man becoming a beast is posed differently. Again we may note a likeness of genre between Kafka's novels and those of Camus; but—what is rarely observed—this likeness of genre may be extended to include not only the narratives of Kafka and Camus, but those of Sartre, Simone de Beauvoir, Alberto Moravia, and Vercors as well. The *Three Exemplary Novels* of Unamuno belong to this genre also—as do Dostoevski's *Letters from the Underworld* and Tolstoi's *Death of Ivan Ilyitch*. There is the disarming directness of the narrative, the reportorial rawness of the events, the hovering of style between comic and pathetic modes; there is the seepage or slow sweat of deep metaphysical anxiety rising to the surface of events, while the events themselves reiterate some "limit-situation" (Jaspers) of the human predicament. This is itself fate-laden, and events serve

mainly to bring it to consciousness rather than elaborate a
plot moving toward Aristotelian climax or purgation. The
climax, if reached at all, comes rather at the point at which
the protagonist's condition is recognized or accepted for what
it is and the reader by the same token accepts it as his own,
as being "wounded from behind" (Kierkegaard). Yet the
factors of existential analysis, maieutic involvement, and "reversal" into choice are differently deployed.

Behind the posturing is the search for the "representative anecdote" of which these narratives and some of the
dramas of the Absurd are mutations or variations. Each existentialist writer is an author in search of his anecdote. In
this quest he risks becoming an epigram of his own questing
or a footnote to his own confession. Kierkegaard becomes a
"Danish *Don Quixote*," or a "*Don Juan* of the Understanding," or a "*Hamlet* of the Infinite." Yet his own representative anecdote was that of Job, or perhaps of Abraham.
Camus chose Sisyphus. Zarathustra would seem to function
in this way for Heidegger. But all three—Kierkegaard, Camus,
Heidegger—are in search of a more ultimate anecdote beyond
the anecdotes of our predicament. Each is seeking, wittingly
or unwittingly, an anecdote of fulfillment. In the literature
expressive of each orientation, we see the representative
anecdote first chosen passing over from predicament to acceptance, from analysis to response. We shall consider these
orientations therefore, and their many mutations, in turn.
For although the classification is somewhat arbitrary (like
Wittgenstein's triangles), these three postulations—the
Kierkegaardian, the Camus-Sartrean, and the Heideggerian
—distribute between them the possibilities for literary theory
and practice as evidenced thus far in contemporary existentialist literature. (Now that the triangle has served its preliminary purpose, I am quite willing to dispense with it, just
as Wittgenstein would kick away the ladder by which he has
climbed!)

II. THE KIERKEGAARDIAN SETTING

"He who does not live either poetically or religiously is a fool!" exclaimed Kierkegaard in his *Concluding Unscientific Postscript.*[6] Kierkegaard sought to live religiously. But this meant apostleship—an accolade one does not confer upon oneself. Apostleship is *given*; it is conferred. By it one becomes an "exception." A poet, or a genius, may be an exception; but in order for this to become a serious matter, in order for the poet to qualify for apostleship, "he himself must be unfree, [must be] forced into the position." It is this being forced into position (by his calling) that constitutes his being "absolutely, paradoxically, teleologically" placed.[7] This is a point of religious suffering: it is "the pain by which he is nailed out in isolation . . . and he must be compelled to it if it is to be a serious matter."[8]

W. H. Auden, following Kierkegaard here, speaks of being

> . . . *Hunted . . . out of life* to play
> At living in some other way. . . .[9]

Kierkegaard aspired to be such a one. Nevertheless he referred to himself again and again as a poet, recognizing that his aesthetic genuis was his greatest talent (hence "temptation"), always drawing him away from the proclamations and martyrdoms of apostleship. His task became thereby a Socratic one—to make men aware "of their own ruin."[10]

[6] Ch. iv, sect. 2a, 2, as noted by Unamuno in *The Tragic Sense of Life* (London: The Macmillan Co., 1921), p. 198.

[7] "The Genius and the Apostle," in *The Present Age*, trans. Alexander Dru and Walter Lowrie (New York: Oxford University Press, 1940), p. 160.

[8] *Journals*, trans. Alexander Dru, (New York: Oxford University Press, 1938), #1135.

[9] *The Double Man* (The New Year Letter), (New York: Random House, 1941), Lines 109–110, notes pp. 84–85.

[10] *Journals* (Dru), #638.

This "ruin" consists in the Self's failure properly to relate itself to "its own self" through "willing to be itself" and thereby grounding itself "transparently in the Power which posited it."[11] Psychologically this is the failure of men rightly to relate themselves to reality—both in themselves and in their situation; religiously it is the failure rightly to relate themselves to God.

In this sense the entire Kierkegaardian dialectic can be understood as a footnote to the *Pensées* of Pascal—on the one hand, the misery of men without God; and on the other, the happiness of men with God. The "genuine subjective existing thinker" is therefore "always as negative as he is positive, and *vice versa*." His mode of communication is made to conform to this condition. "He is conscious of the negativity of the infinite in existence, and he constantly *keeps the wound of the negative open*, which in the bodily realm is sometimes *the condition for a cure*" (italics added).

Since this notation is made by Kierkegaard with reference to the maieutic art of communication, it is worth noting his concluding comment: such a thinker "is therefore never a teacher but a learner; and since he is always just as negative as he is positive, he is always striving."[12]

This perspective is common to most existentialist literature. It is important therefore to emphasize the key points in it and the implications for language and the modes of communication.

What Kierkegaard calls the "negativity of the infinite in existence" is Pascal's recognition that "nothing stays for us"; that the groundwork of every supposed security in life "cracks" beneath our feet and "opens to abysses": it is his recognition of "the infinite within" and the "infinite without," of the indefinable present within an infinite past and

---

11 *The Sickness unto Death*, trans. Walter Lowrie (Princeton: Princeton University Press, 1941), p. 19.

12 *Concluding Unscientific Postscript*, p. 78.

an infinite future. But it is also Sartre's "hole" in things, through which any permanence "leaks" away. It is also the "nothingness which noughts" in both Sartre and Heidegger. It is the root of Pascal's "terror," of Kierkegaard's "dread," of Heidegger's "anguish," and of Sartre's "nausea." It is that perpetual task of becoming what one is and of being what one is becoming that obliges every man to live in advance of himself. This is both a challenge and a risk, which men therefore seek to avoid. In the evasion lurks the ruin. Man stands in contradiction to himself. Kafka put it deftly: "A man was astonished how easily he went the eternal way; he happened to be rushing backwards along it."[13] In terms of the Creation myth, it resumes, as Auden notes, the plight of Adam:

> Since Adam, being free to choose,
> Chose to imagine he was free
> To choose his own necessity,
> Lost in his freedom, Man pursues
> The shadow of his images. . . .[14]

Rilke too is Kierkegaardian when, in his "Eighth Elegy," he wistfully inquires:

> Who's turned us round like this, so that we always
> do what we may, retain the attitude
> of someone who's departing? Just as he,
> on the last hill, that shows him all his valley
> for the last time, will turn and stop and linger,
> we live our lives, for ever taking leave.[15]

No literature is so conscious of this central ambivalence of the self as is the existentialist literature, or the literature

13 *Aphorisms*, "Reflctions on Sin, Pain, Hope, and the True Way," #35: in *The Great Wall of China*, trans. Willa and Edwin Muir (New York: Shocken Books, 1937), p. 286.

14 W. H. Auden, "For the Time Being, A Christmas Oratorio," in *The Collected Poetry of W. H. Auden* (New York: Random House, 1945), p. 420.

15 *Duino Elegies*, VIII, lines 70–75, trans. J. B. Leishman and Stephen Spender (New York: W. W. Norton & Company, 1939), p. 71.

affected by existentialist thought. Existentialist literature exploits the conditions of cleavage within the self, thus keeping the wound of the negative open: it does this in the belief that, or in the hope that, this is often the condition for a cure. Or (as with Camus) it will do it in the simple belief that it is better to face up to the brute facts of the human condition than to go on contriving illusions, religious or metaphysical, about ourselves and the world around us.

From this arises the interesting fact that existentialist literature tends to be aphoristic, epigrammatic, ironic or parabolic—drawing the reader into recognitions of the ambivalent nature of the human predicament and into confrontations thereby with himself as a subject and protagonist of that predicament. Existentialist literature similarly tends toward parable—whether extended into full-length narrative or contracted into epigram or aphorism. For this reason the reader or spectator is not provided with "results" or resolutions, but is often left holding the conundrum or riddle in his hands; or, if resolutions *are* provided, the *denouéments* are often ironic or riddling, though they are sometimes hortatory (as in Camus's *Caligula* or Ionesco's *Rhinoceros*). They require a response from the reader or spectator in the form of a decision or an action.

Since this is a central characteristic of existentialist literature generally, we shall do well to consider a specific instance. It may be seen most clearly in the work of Franz Kafka.

III. KAFKA

The work of Franz Kafka is remarkable in many respects, not the least of which is the manner in which one moves so easily from his aphorisms to his parables to his great narratives and back again as though the former were but the latter condensed.

In his "Aphorisms" we read:

> He has the feeling that merely by being alive he is blocking his own way. From this sense of hindrance, again, he deduces the proof that he is alive.

Again:

> The bony structure of his own forehead blocks his way; he batters himself bloody against his own forehead.[16]

From this one moves easily to the descriptive lines of *The Burrow*, in which we see the nucleus of the foregoing aphorisms expounded into a parable:

> With my brow I ran against the earth, day and night, a thousand times; I was happy when I had beaten it bloody, for this was proof that the wall had begun to become firm. . . .

This surprising narrative goes on for some seventy pages describing the construction of an underground keep, its tortuous and labyrinthine passages, its systems of deception and defense, the mounting anxieties that attend upon the narrator's life within it. He becomes aware of imperfections in his work and his uneasiness grows. One day he hears a noise, which is repeated more and more frequently. He ventures upon occasional sorties into the world outside; but "duty" and "security" recall him to his burrow. The threat of "the Enemy" increases as "Something," some "animal," seems to tunnel closer and closer toward the center of his keep.

Is this a narrative dealing with the relationship between mind and reality, as has been suggested? Or is it subtler than this? Does not its extraordinary fascination consist in the psychological adequacy with which the narrative lays hold upon every man's tendency to hide from reality, to seek "comfort" and "security" from reality by building up elaborate systems of illusion and rationalization against its de-

16 "Aphorisms," in *The Great Wall of China*, pp. 264–265.

mands? "Comfort" had led to the burrow's being built. It was a product of fear and lassitude, guaranteed by the sophistication of its intricate escape patterns. But the escape from reality is gradually overtaken by reality itself, which comes upon it like a threat from the outside. This brings on the mounting anxieties and the confession of the burrow's architect that he has failed to conquer reality because he has failed to live reality. Reality takes on the characteristics of death invading the central keep of the body as well as of the psyche. The narrator confesses an increasing loss of faith in his own sophistications of defense. It is possible as these doubts increase that the narrator might experience that narrow escape into the world of fact which is sometimes brought on by the threat of reality. The story is not finished. Its outcome (as a story) we do not know. Its outcome depends upon us, upon our choosing. The narrative, like the Enemy it describes, has worked its way past our own unconscious defenses: we are left with the risk in our hands—the choice between reality and the sham solutions within which we seek to hide from it.

It is much the same in *The Metamorphosis*. "As Gregor Samsa awoke one morning from a troubled dream, he found himself changed in his bed to some monstrous kind of vermin." He was, in fact, a giant cockroach. The narrative pursues the embarrassments attendant upon this transformation, introducing once again the unconscious motivations behind human behavior. Each morning Samsa had experienced a desire to return to the inorganic and had experienced guilt feelings for thus wishing to desert humanity; yet the cumulative power of these feelings seemed to be carrying him "as on a train" toward some indefinable but ultimate catastrophe—the metamorphosis itself.

This same motif has been noted in Dostoevski's penchant for insects and spiders, which possibly imply an awakening of conscience revealing the compulsive tug towards bestiality, as well as an awakening to change with its attendant movement towards death. "I declare to you solemnly," says one of Dostoevski's characters, "that many times I have wanted to become an insect. . . . I swear to you, gentlemen, that too much conscience is a sickness, a real and proper sickness. . . ." In *The Idiot*, Nature—not conscience—is assigned the bestial role—"an immense, merciless, dumb beast . . . an enormous, and repugnant spider." In the case of Gregory Samsa the fear of death is an emergent awareness. It penetrates the bourgeois sense of "security" and slowly builds up a smothered but smoldering hatred of the cockroach on the part of those about him. As in Tolstoi's *The Death of Ivan Ilyitch* the fundamental deceitfulness of public and social attitudes, to say nothing of the affections of those about us, is revealed. When the cockroach finally dies, everyone is openly or secretly relieved and everything becomes "normal" again. But once again, as in *The Burrow*, we have been led into "the mysterious controlling center"—into the psyche, into *my* life, and the paradox of all significant "knowing" is made plain: namely, that only through transformation itself is any authentic knowledge of this deep center of the self revealed. The negative parable has opened up the positive possibility of transformation in the "spirit."

The same is true of Kafka's doctrinal aphorisms. "A cage went in search of a bird," he writes, in a startling paradox that is almost a riddle. But it is a riddle the answer to which is already known to us secretly, even though we may refuse to permit the secret to come into conscious awareness. It is the secret of our freedom. For man (Kafka's "He" of the "Aphorisms") "is divided against himself." He is thirsty, and yet he is separated from a spring only by a clump of bushes. One part of him overlooks the whole and sees that he is standing beside a spring; but the other part sees nothing, and since he ignores what the first part sees (knows), he does not drink. So with our freedom. Life's structures, cagelike, seek to enclose us (the bird). More baffling still, we ourselves seem always to be going in search of a cage (the "comfort" and "security" of the burrow, for example), and feel progressively imprisoned, for we have "no conception of freedom."

> But it was a barred cage that he was in. . . . (Yet) the prisoner was really free, he could take part in everything, nothing that went on outside escaped him, he could simply have left the cage, the bars were yards apart, he was not even a prisoner.[17]

This paradox is parlayed by Kafka into the short parable of "The Knock at the Manor Gate." While riding by the great house with his sister on the way home, his *sister* (not even he himself) knocked or gestured toward knocking on the gate as they passed. The people were terrified, and warned them that "the proprietor" of the manor "would charge [them] with it" and "the interrogation would begin immediately." Horsemen came riding after them. The sister went on home to attire herself more suitably. The brother was taken ("the important thing seemed their having found me"); he was brought before the judge, and under the sharp scrutinizing eyes of the officials (cf. Sartre's "the Other" and his "Look") he undertook his statement of defense. The more he said the more the room resembled a prison cell: and the question gradually emerged as to whether "any other air than prison air" would be endurable for him now.

We now have both *The Trial* and *The Castle* (The Manor) in miniature. The two novels lift the little parables into their full-blown dimensions, exhibiting the ambivalence of human behavior at the point where it reaches its ultimate encounters. Religiously speaking, we encounter the Justice of God in the one and the problem of Grace in the other. In the one case we come into the world—each one of us innocently concealed within the mystery of his own origin —and then, like Joseph K., "without having done anything

17 *Ibid.*, pp. 281, 275, 264.

wrong [we are] arrested one fine morning" and hurried off
to the Interrogation Chamber.

> Then a shout came from the next room which made him start
> so violently that his teeth rattled against the glass. "The Inspector
> wants to see you," was its tenor. . . .

We have come athwart the Law. Everything that Joseph K.
attempts in his own defense only complicates his status and
compounds his guilt, and though he never does see the judge
and never stands in the High Court, he is finally condemned
and his life is required of him. It is absurd, of course. Kafka's
narrative has much of the ludicrous objectivity of *Alice in
Wonderland*. The common sense of Joseph K. is again and
again overborne by the imperturbable logic of a comical
officialdom. But it is our world and our comedy played out
to the gag line of the absurd and ludicrous jest. Again
theologically, it is the mystery of Original Sin and what
Kafka calls "the eternal recapitulation of the occurrence."[18]

> The original sin [writes Kafka] . . . consists in the complaint,
> which man makes and never ceases making, that a wrong has been
> done to him, that the original sin was once committed upon
> him.[19]

This is the precise pattern of the Job complaint, of
whom Joseph K. is the quasi-comic refraction—as though
Kierkegaard had grasped Job's lightning in fear and trembling and passed it on to Kafka as a tingling dialectical
charade.

But Kafka's central view is contained in the more penetrating aphorism[20] in which he notes:

> We are sinful not merely because we have eaten of the Tree
> of Knowledge, but also because we have not yet eaten of the Tree
> of Life. The state in which we find ourselves is sinful, quite in-
> dependent of guilt.

18 *Ibid.*, #62, p. 293.
19 *Ibid.*, "He," p. 270.
20 *Ibid.*, #79, p. 298.

That is the heart of Kafka, and it is the core also of much of W. H. Auden's later poetry.[21]

The Castle, obviously, is the other side of this coin. Here is the attempt to establish some communication with the high Authority, to acquire vocation, to eat of the Tree of Life. But—again, the "Aphorisms"—"there is a goal, but no way; what we call the way is only wavering."[22] All of K.'s attempts to make contact with the Castle are thwarted. The Authority is not at the discretion of our petitions. Grace is not forthcoming by reason of our strife after it. We cannot force the Kingdom: the Kingdom comes. "Before God we are always in the wrong," as Kierkegaard put it. Our effort, wrongly premised spiritually, is repellent to Grace. Nor is Grace compliant with or coerced by our law, as the episode of the Barnabas family shows.

All this was rehearsed by Kierkegaard in his *Fear and Trembling* where the problem of Abraham's sacrifice of Isaac was propounded and the question of "a teleological suspension of the ethical" was raised. There is no doubt that, in the Christian view, the "ethics of Grace" (as Berdyaev called it) transcends the "ethics of the law." The latter in its Pharisaical, normative or legalistic forms is inimical even to the "good" of many ethical systems. But Kafka plays with this existential discrepancy, exhibiting its absurd and "irrational" forms (when viewed from within the perspectives of our ethical norms). "For the Castle gentlemen everything is possible," said Olga. "What do we know of the thoughts of these gentlemen?"[23]

---

[21] An extensive treatment of the existentialist perspectives in Auden's poetry would be appropriate here, though his uses of Pascal, Kierkegaard, Freud, Kafka, Nietzsche, Jung, Niebuhr, Tillich, etc., can be readily noted. His aphoristic talent is also apparent; and he has expounded the view that there are only two kinds of art, escapist art and parable art (a distinction not unlike the terms "frivolous" and "serious" as used by Kierkegaard).

[22] "Aphorisms," in *The Great Wall of China,* p. 283.

[23] *The Castle,* trans. Edwin and Willa Muir (New York: Alfred A. Knopf, 1943), pp. 265, 252.

Muir calls *The Castle* a religious allegory, comparing it with Bunyan's Pilgrim, with the "reservation . . . that the 'progress' of the pilgrim will here remain in question. . . ."[24] It is a big question! Bunyan's Pilgrim has a clear goal, "knows what the necessary moves are," and an indubitable road on which to travel—thanks to a "banally simplified theological system [existing] full-blown before it." The same would be true of Dante, with a *highly* sophisticated theological system existing full-blown before him. The crucial difference here is that in our time no such "system" may be presupposed: rather its *absence* characterizes the journey. Therefore "there is a goal, but no way . . . ." The "allegory" is thus an allegory of inwardness, in which we probe by a necessary but unwarranted quest the "negativity of the infinite in existence," and do so with the smiling knowledge (how immaculately adroit is Kafka's humor!) that the whims of the gods—the sorties of Grace—are somehow (we cannot appraise them, we only experience them) benevolent and fitting within the proprieties of the divine humor.

The term "humor" assigned here is in obvious contrast with the grotesque pettifogging and pompous pettiness of the Castle bureaucracy—an inflated Austrian "department," officials swamped in documents and "red tape," spawning subordinates who are smothered with procedures and too much hastening hither and yon (like Tweedledum and Tweedledee), too top-heavy with the sobrieties of organization to be more than casually concerned with the trivial affairs of the people. Who can doubt that Kafka is deftly satirizing the entire ecclesiastical and hierarchical talent of the human race—the complex of patterns and dignities which we so grandiosely interpose betwixt ourselves and the simplicities of Grace—the fallacy of misplaced discreteness (to paraphrase a noble and learned cliche), closing out God with the substitution of our own protective projections. Klamm—

24 *Ibid.*, p. iii.

who comes nearest to representing the Divine (in "his re-
moteness, . . . his impregnable dwelling, . . . his silence, . . .
his downward pressing gaze, . . . which could never be proved
or disproved, . . . etc.") is clearly beyond "protocol." No
one knows his real appearance: he appears one way when he
enters the village, and another when he leaves it, and "he's
almost another person up at the Castle." Accounts of his
appearance differ: as to his height, his bearing, and the cut
of his beard. All accounts agree, however, that he always
wears "a black morningcoat with long tails." What one sees
depends "on the mood of the observer. . . . A man like
Klamm who is so much sought after and so rarely seen is
apt to take different shapes in people's imagination."[25] Perhaps the most indicative statement in the narrative comes
when K. forces a showdown with one of the two "assistants"
who have been assigned to help him. "What, then," asks K.,
"have you to complain about?" "That you can't understand
a joke," is the reply; and the "assistant" goes on to explain
that "the main thing" in their assignment was "to cheer
him up a little . . . . he takes everything too seriously."[26]

The narrative is unfinished. It has "no result," as Kierkegaard would say. Max Brod reports that Kafka once told
him that K. "was not to relax his struggle, but was to die
worn out from it"; at his deathbed a message was to come
from the Castle granting him leave to live and to work in
the village. Brod concludes from this that *The Castle* thereby
echoes Goethe's *Faust*: "whoever keeps on striving, him we
may save." But it would seem that just the opposite inference
should be drawn: namely, that not through striving is Grace
to be won. Striving must pass over into acceptance. We are

25 *Ibid.*, pp. 152, 228–229, 235. *Klamm*, in German, is an adjective meaning light, close, narrow, hard, compact, scarce, clammy! In *The Castle* this
ephemeral, omnipresent and ludicrous figure is "God" as reported and defined
by humankind generally. It is the dramatized euphemism of our God projections, drawn in such humorous delineation as to make it plain that the
"God beyond 'God' " bears scant resemblance to our deified images.

26 *Ibid.*, p. 300.

strangers by reason of our strife with reality and with ourselves and by reason of our struggle to force the Kingdom.
We must learn to be and to let be. "The positive is already
given," says Kafka. "What is laid upon us is to accomplish
the negative."[27]

This is, in effect, to negate our will to negation: to let
Grace happen, to discover that the Kingdom comes, that
"the Garden" *is*—to use a pertinent figure of Auden's. Is it
not this which led Kafka to repeat to Max Brod the Flaubert
anecdote in which Flaubert, after visiting a family—happy,
buoyant, the mother surrounded by "her brood of lovely
children"—muttered passionately on the way home: *"Ils sont
dans le vrai!"* (They are [living] in the true)? *D'être dans
le vrai*—to be in the true and right of life: this is the prized
"authenticity" of existentialist philosophy. What Kafka's
parables of the right and the good depict is that which is
pathetic and comical in the discrepancy that exists between
God and man by reason of man's obstinate inability to live
in the right and to acquiesce in the true. Man imposes his
requirements upon the Godhead and demands a response
on his own terms. Thus he projects his images and believes
himself deceived when they cut him off from "the divine."[28]

IV. FROM KIERKEGAARD TO SARTRE

In this first panel of works—the Kierkegaardian orientation—we have included Dostoevski, *The Death of Ivan
Ilyitch* of Tolstoi, Kierkegaard himself, Kafka, Unamuno,

---

27 "Aphorisms," #24, *op. cit.*, p. 284.

28 The parables of Unamuno, his *Three Exemplary Novels* for example,
exhibit the same discrepancy. In Unamuno the tragic and pathetic side (as
against the comical) is characteristic. Yet, as in Kafka, the style hovers between agony and whimsy; there is the same deceitful simplicity of narrative,
the same adroit unconcealing of the deeper meaning, the same running in-
nuendo of the reader's complicity in the unspecified universal crime, the same
necessity for reading them the second time—from the end, so to speak, after
the riddle has been propounded and in the light of another and acquired
perspective.

and W. H. Auden. These are all writers in whom the otherness of God is still felt acutely, or in whose work His absence has still the sustaining effect of a Presence, even though, as with Kafka, His transcendence is such as to remove Him from all approachability from the human side. The ambivalence of man and the ambiguity of the human situation is seen clearly by all of these writers. What begins as an existential discrepancy between the "absconded self" (Auden) and its authentic self-understanding becomes a discrepancy between the self and the otherness of God. This is developed with exquisite irony in Kafka, with extreme pathos in Unamuno, with dialectical wit and dogmatic candor in Auden. Its existential analysis conforms to Pascal's "misery without God" as well as to the several patterns of *divertissement* disclosed in the *Pensées* and in Kierkegaard's *Stages on Life's Way*. We should also note accretions and parallels from Freud, from depth psychology, and from biblical realism.

This latter factor is, indeed, so basic to existentialism in all its forms that one must consider that the emergence of existential awareness in Western thought bears witness to the breaking through of Judeo-Christian perspectives after their long suppression under substantialistic, intellectualistic, and rationalistic thought forms. For this reason the Job drama becomes the representative anecdote of existentialism in its Kierkegaardian forms. Socrates becomes its archetypal thinker from antiquity and Pascal from modern times. This is not to overlook the place of other archetypal figures (such as Abraham, Don Juan, Faust, the Wandering Jew, etc., in Kierkegaard's thought), but to note, rather, the summation properties and the ubiquity of the one image over the others. Formally, of course, and perhaps secretly, it is Christ Himself and the divine drama of redemption which is central, either as a renewing presence or as vital absence. For Kierkegaard Christ is *the paradigm*. "He is the paradigm in the situation of contemporaneousness . . . . every generation has to begin all over again with Christ and thus to present His life as the paradigm."[29] Other paradigms are derivative of *this* paradigm. *This* paradigm functions both absolutely and existentially.

> . . . it draws attention to itself, and then it presents a contra-diction. There is something which makes it impossible for one to desist from looking—and lo! while one looks, one sees as in a mirror, one gets to see oneself, or He, the sign of the contradiction, sees into the depths of one's heart while one is gazing into the contradiction. A contradiction placed directly in front of a man— if only one can get him to look upon it—is a mirror; while he is judging, what dwells within him must be revealed. It is *a riddle*, but while he is guessing, what dwells within him is revealed by how he guesses. The contradiction puts before him a choice, and while he is choosing, he himself is revealed.[30]

This paragraph is in many respects the dogmatic center of Kierkegaard's Christianity. The God-man is for him the sign of the contradiction; but for this very reason direct communication is an impossibility for Him—the God-Man. He cannot communicate Himself directly, but must elicit from "the Learner" that response to ultimacy which is the learner's "choice of absolute significance." The learner must be led into this moment of choosing, this moment of recognition—a coming to himself in response to the power which posited him. Literature may present parables of this journey, it may present the contradiction *negatively,* it may dialec-tically cross-question the learner *out* of his supposed fixed knowledges and pseudo-security patterns, it may riddle him this riddle of the paradigm of paradigms, it may riddle him the Riddle to which he must himself *become* the answer, it may lead him to the "place of meeting" (Buber)—but it must

---

29 *Training in Christianity* (New York: Oxford University Press, 1941), pp. 109–111.

30 *Ibid.,* p. 126, italics added.

leave him there holding "the Night of the Absolute" in his hands.

This is the mystical moment in Kierkegaard's dialectic. It is described in a *Journal* entry written in the year preceding his death in 1855, under the caption: "The Night of the Absolute."

> Man has a natural dread of walking in the dark—what wonder then that he naturally has a dread of the absolute, of having to do with the absolute, of which it is true that no night and "no deepest gloom is half so dark" as this gloom and this night, where all relative ends (the common milestones and sign-posts), where all relative considerations (the lanterns which are normally a help to us), where even the tenderest and sincerest feelings of devotion— are quenched . . . for otherwise it is not unconditionally absolute.[31]

This is the moment to which the Kierkegaardian dialectic must bring us; for the "Stages," while "severely ontological" as Baron von Hugel claimed, are not substantialistically so, but are inwardly and psychologically so. They are an analysis of the either/or of acceptance or defiance of the human situation when set against its ultimate conditions. The *ambiguity* of the Kierkegaardian existentialism is of another kind. It is a case of "the Stuttering Bishop"— the halting tergiversation between subjective appropriation in inwardness and capitulation to traditional doctrine. Kierkegaard is clear when he speaks of the God-man as a mirror; he is the puppet of his conditioning when he makes polemical concessions to doctrines of the atonement and the like. But dogmatic appeals, in Kierkegaard, remain "acoustical illusions."

Auden put it bluntly (in his whimsical "Academic Graffiti") :

> Søren Kierkegaard
> Tried awfully hard

[31] *Journals*, #1308, p. 499.

> To take The Leap,
> But fell in a heap.

Auden is perhaps more *gauche* than clever in this remark; but the verse exhibits nevertheless the point at which existentialism on Kierkegaardian terms may remain caught in the substantialistic matrix of dogma. Kierkegaard knows quite well that "Christianity is not a doctrine."[32] He knows that "faith is the objective uncertainty due to the repulsion of the absurd held fast by the passion of inwardness." Nevertheless in "reintroducing Christianity into Christendom" he is constantly tempted to turn the "leap of faith" (away from objective certainties) into the objective idolization of "the Paradox," the God-man, the affirmation of the Contradiction as a postulate instead of an eternal becoming (i.e., a perpetual appropriation by way of a constant repetition of the movement in faith).

This ambivalence in Kierkegaard extends itself in a variety of forms to the existentialist literature arising out of this perspective. It appears as a nonaesthetic intrusion of dogma into the literary piece as stultifying in kind as the intrusion of propaganda or moralizing against which the artist—Auden, for example—is so thoroughly set. But it helps to account for the fact that the existentialist literature (in this kind) remains, or tends to remain, intellectualistic—excelling in the forms of the riddle, the joke, the epigram, wit, irony, conceit, and the rationalistic revels of dialectic —so confining its pathos (Unamuno excepted) to the pathos of "the absurd." Its parabolic seriousness (Adam, Abraham, Job, Socrates, Don Quixote, Falstaff, Faust, etc.) is seldom realized: and when realized it is realized as Problem rather than as Mystery (to employ Marcel's distinction).

The realization of the absurd "constitutes the notification" that ethical despair has been broken through and "the

---

32 *Training in Christianity*, p. 108.

leap" may be "posited," which leads Kierkegaard to a statement that anticipates Kafka's work most significantly.

> . . . the repetition [Kierkegaard's term for the subjective realization of a new immediacy with the truth] itself is a movement *in virtue of the absurd,* and the teleological suspension *a trial.* The concept of a "trial" corresponds again to the fact that the religious paradigm is an irregularity (as opposed to the ethical norm of the universal). From the ethical point of view a trial is unthinkable, since it is precisely by always being valid that the ethical is universally valid. For the religious paradigm a trial is the highest earnest; from the merely ethical point of view a trial is a jest, and the notion of *existing* on trial is so far from being earnest that it is a comic *motif* which conceivably enough no poet has yet used to represent want of will in an almost insane maximum.[33]

No poet, that is, until Kafka—though Kierkegaard himself presented Job's venture as a trial. The trial of K. is certainly a jest from the purely normative point of view; but from the standpoint of the religious paradigm it is the highest earnest. The religious paradigm, in short, is just the opposite of the universal—it is the exception *beyond* the universal. Indeed it *breaks through* the universal, whereas the classical hero expressed "the regular conformity of the universal in his mode of declension."[34] Now follows Kierkegaard's dialectical *coup de grace,* so far as this argument is concerned: ". . . the fact that the highest earnestness of the religious life is *recognizable by the jest,* is like the paradigm being an irregularity or particularity, and God's omnipresence His invisibility, and revelation a mystery."[35]

We note here two things: (1) the *disclosure* of religious seriousness by way of the jest (which is itself an analogue of the function of the work of art), and (2) the paradox of the God-relation: namely, that His very presence conceals Him, and His self-disclosure remains at the same time a mystery. Therefore, the art of communication becomes the

---

[33] *Concluding Unscientific Postscript,* p. 235.
[34] *Ibid.,* p. 231.
[35] *Ibid.,* p. 235, italics added.

art of taking away, as Kierkegaard says;[36] the Socratic maieutic art, *which makes the reader himself active,* does not provide solutions adjusted to the modes of the universal, but "ends in a sting."[37] If the situation of Job is being presented, it must be so presented as to challenge the spectator: its question must be a question directed to me.[38] The poet's *style,* with its subjective concern, must "be as manifold as the opposites he holds in combination."[39] The classical (abstract) forms will fail, since the form must relate itself "first and last" to existence, and will have all possibilities —the poetical, the ethical, the dialectical, and the religious —at its disposal.[40] He has "only a single scene, existence"— "inwardness in existing as a human being"—the concreteness of which is achieved through "bringing the existential categories into relationship with one another."[41] Like Socrates, he knows that behind the negative disclosure (at which point he arrives) the positive resides: Socrates did not know what this positive element was, hence his ignorance; Kierkegaard knows it as the Paradox apprehended through "the leap" of faith.

What is disconcerting in Kierkegaard is that this "Paradox" so often functions merely as an idea, as the sign of "the unhappy consciousness," and is experienced only negatively—i.e., as the last antinomy of the intellect. Undoubtedly there is for Kierkegaard a Being with whom we must be *en rapport,* a Being which is *for us* when we stand within this rapport; but unhappily (and ironically) this is for Kierkegaard (in his doctrinal hyperbole, at least) a Being with whom we are *unable to be* in any rapport.[42] Since Kierkegaard

36 *Ibid.,* p. 245.
37 *Journals* (Dru), #578, p. 155.
38 *Concluding Unscientific Postscript,* p. 321.
39 *Ibid.,* p. 319.
40 *Ibid.,* p. 320.
41 *Ibid.*
42 Cf. Jean Wahl, *Études Kierkegaardiennes* (Paris: Librarie Philosophique J. Vrin, 1949), p. 451.

cannot accept this Paradox, and so remains "unhappily in love with God," the Paradox becomes an antinomy intellectually perceived but not existentially resolved. The aesthetic reflex of this is that his "imagination" (of which he fears he has too much) becomes "fantasy"; and fantasy comes, as he himself points out, not *before* the dialectic, but *after* the dialectic and therefore is "not immediate." For this reason Kierkegaard remains a poet by the grace of irony, and the literature produced under his "sign" exploits the ironic forms—wit, epigram, riddle, jest, conceit, and parable moving toward allegory, dialectic.

The novel is the predominant mode of literature in this Kierkegaardian phase, along with some poetry. It has produced very little drama, though the "Theater of the Absurd" is foreshadowed in it. It is, perhaps, the covert intellectualism of his Paradox, which—demoting imagination to the status of fantasy—deters the poet and leaves the dramatist holding fast to the negativity of the infinite in the ironic play of wit in its existential *reductio ad absurdum.*

This would mean that a Kierkegaardian aesthetic would tend, on this point, to remain *classical*: that is, its theory of the imagination is undeveloped and effects no displacement of traditional modes. The *dialectic* comes first, and is intellectualistic; *imagination* comes second, is dependent, and (since it establishes nothing, but only adorns or manipulates) it functions as *fantasy.* Just as for Aristotle *metaphor* is an adornment and not a primary mode of laying hold upon the real, so for Kierkegaard imagination is dependent and adjectival and is not a mode of primary relation ("immediacy") with the real.

V. THE SARTREAN PERSPECTIVE
IN LITERATURE

Drama emerges in the second, or Sartrean, phase along with the novel. This drama retains the characteristics of the irony of the Absurd of which we have just been speaking, and eventuates in negative disclosure. Indeed, the "Theater of the Absurd"—Beckett, Adamov, Ionesco, Genet, Arrabel, Pinter, etc.—is its logical outcome. God is no longer a Presence or a presupposition of the narrative or dramatic scene. The rationalistic stance of Descartes—transferred to the "lucidity" of immediate perceptions—replaces the existential awareness of Pascal; the willed ego of Stoicism replaces the ignorance of Socrates; and the Myth of Sisyphus (by way of Camus) displaces the anecdote of Job as the representative anecdote. Meanwhile, the strategies of Kierkegaard's "Stages" are replaced by Sartre's existential analysis with its new set of metaphors and catchwords—nausea, viscosity, the hole, the stare, the body, bad faith, freedom, nothingness, the role, Being, the Self, Transcendence, absurdity, and death.

Before examining these metaphors, however, it is important to acknowledge a certain aura of suspicion that lies over French existentialism of the Sartrean brand. It is a suspicion of role-playing, of sham or covert duplicity. According to a Swiss journalist (who lives in Paris) the case of Jean-Paul Sartre is "an extreme case of . . . literary inflation."[43] Simone de Beauvoir remarked concerning Sartre in his boyhood years: "He was particularly happy when he could not understand what he was writing."[44] It is further alleged that there is a certain "void" at the heart of Sartre's astonishing literary output which can only be understood when that literature is seen as Sartre in search of himself. But it is also possible that the suspicion of role-playing is due to Sartre's having had to fulfill "the exhausting assignment of being the Sartre he had not invented."[45] Or perhaps

---

[43] Herbert Lüthy, "The Void of Jean-Paul Sartre," in *The Anchor Review*, #2 (Garden City: Doubleday Anchor Books, 1957), p. 243.

[44] *Harper's Bazaar*, 1946 (pp. 113, 158, 160); quoted in H. Spiegelberg, *The Phenomenological Movement, A Historical Introduction* (The Hague: Martinus Nijhoff, 1960), vol. ii, p. 447.

[45] Lüthy, *op. cit.*, pp. 243–244.

the Sartre he did invent became a public commitment and so a convention he could not resign.

However this may be, Sartre (over and above his talents as philosopher) is an astute literary critic, a voracious novelist, and a talented playwright. As critic, he probes with the skill of a surgeon, cutting cleanly to the malignancy, exposing it deftly, and then (as often as not) leaving it for the patient and his attendants to clear up as best they may. What one of the Goncourt brothers remarked of Sainte-Beuve might better be applied to Sartre: "When I hear [him], with his little phrases, touch a dead man, I think I see a swarm of ants invading a corpse: he cleans up a glory in ten minutes, and leaves the illustrious gentleman only a neat skeleton."[46]

Sartre praises Camus's *The Stranger,* but lauds its classical order and tone rather than its existential adequacy, and then places its author nearer to Voltaire than to Kafka, Camus's chief inspirer. Faulkner's humanism, he writes, "is probably the only acceptable kind"; but "doesn't he realize that his great, dark figures are only facades? Is he taken in by his own art?" And again, after accusing François Mauriac of playing God with his characters, he concludes that "M. Mauriac is not a novelist. . . . [He] has put himself first. He has chosen divine omniscience and omnipotence. But novels are written *by* men and *for* men. In the eyes of God, Who cuts through appearances and goes beyond them, there is no novel, no art, for art thrives on appearances. God is not an artist. Neither is M. Mauriac."[47]

Doubtless Sartre is here imposing a little on the credulity of his readers if he—a man who does not believe in God—expects his readers to credit his theological exclusion of God from the realms of poetry. But the important sen-

---

[46] Quoted in George M. Harper, *Charles-Augustin Saint-Beuve* (Philadelphia: J. P. Lippincott Co., 1909), p. 295.

[47] See Jean-Paul Sartre, *Literary Essays* (New York: Philosophical Library, 1957), pp. 41, 78, 23.

tence precedes the omniscient ones. "Novels are written *by* men and *for* men," he says. Here the Sartrean aesthetic emerges. Although (as he has remarked elsewhere) "the problems which the present age poses can be treated abstractly by philosophical reflection. . . . we whose purpose it is to live those problems" should "sustain our thinking by those imaginative and concrete experiences which are novels."[48] Sartre's literary work may here be seen to parallel his formal philosophical studies much as Kierkegaard's pseudonymous masks supply mouthpieces for his dialectic.

Three of Sartre's basic themes will serve to illuminate his approach to literature as philosophy.

First, his humanism is thoroughgoing. The "death-of-God" thesis implies not merely that there is no God to be thought of as over against us sustaining an order we have to discover, and so guaranteeing the objectivity of Truth as an ordered hierarchy of values on which to base a calendar of moral judgments; it means that the "objectivity" of classical rationalism is refused *in toto* as an evasion of the real. There is no intellectualistic adequation of the thing to the intellect which permits thought to preside over life, just as there is no ineffable world of "essences" or "forms" or "ideas" which are real as over against a world of things which are "appearances." In classicism, life is subordinated to thought, and life's goals are rational and contemplative; in existentialism, thought is instrumental to life, and life must be lived. It is not formula, equation, or system.

In the second place, the notion of the Self is deprived (by the foregoing) of its substantialistic core. The Self is not an object, a thing which may become the object of a formal search, and so be uncovered in its substantiality. It cannot lay its "finger" upon itself as the object of its own inquiry, but remains (in this sense) a "nothingness" (a no-thing-ness) never included in the processes of self-objectification, yet always "present" as the presupposition of the Self's making an object of itself. It has indeed this aspect of being what Sartre calls "in-itself," which, bluntly, is everything that it experiences—matter, pain, memory, the objects it "knows," etc.

But there is another dimension to "Self": there is a "consciousness" within the Self which has the power to separate itself from the in-itself, to nihilate what it is on behalf of what it is not. This is the "for-itself," which "is what it is not, and is not what it is." This "for-itself" is the root of man's freedom. Freedom is not something man *has*: it is something that he *is*. It "signifies simply: autonomy of choice."[49] And while this freedom is radical, the "for-itself" is nevertheless always "engaged" in the world about us, and related to the contingencies of the "in-itself." The ambivalence of the Self consists in the fact that in nihilating the what-it-is of the in-itself it is enabled to project what it is not, thereby asserting the calling of the in-itself to become what it is not. The dynamic interplay of the for-itself with the in-itself perpetually posits the synthesis of the Self as a "project" to be attained. The Self desires to be an in-itself-for-itself (the definition of God, or Sartre tricked out in Hegel's feathers) ; but this it never achieves (though this is what it perpetually desires), for the moment of any particular existential synthesis is the starting point for a fresh nihilating and projecting. The Self is therefore always in advance of itself. Its characteristic is not primarily thought but action. It is of the very "nature" of man that he has no "essence" to be defined objectively, but he is perpetually in the process of freely making himself what he is to be.

The effect of these two theses—the nonexistence of God

or a Rational Order behind the world of "appearances" and the nonexistence of a rational Ego or Substantialistic Self—leads to the third Sartrean thesis: the disclosure of the Absurd. This is what we are left with when our "logic" fails, when the systems and structures of thought erected by the analytical consciousness between our "Selves" and the "abyss" of the noncapturable universe fall away as so many masks at the carnival when the play is ended. Camus has expressed it well:

> A world that one can explain even with bad reasons is a familiar world. But in a universe deprived suddenly both of its illusions and its lights, man feels himself to be a stranger. This exile is without appeal. . . . This divorce between man and his life, the actor and his setting, is properly the feeling of absurdity.[50]

The playwright, Ionesco (in an essay on Kafka), also puts it well:

> The absurd is that which is devoid of purpose . . . cut off from his religious, metaphysical, and transcendental roots, man is lost: all his actions become senseless, absurd, useless.[51]

The French dramatists—Ionesco, Samuel Beckett, Arthur Adamov, Jean Genet—have penetrated this notion of the Absurd very deeply; but Camus has seen it most steadily. "My reasoning wants to be faithful to the evidence that aroused it. That evidence is the absurd." There must be no masking of the evidence. "It is essential to know whether one can live with it." That is the whole question for Camus. Heidegger, he notes, seeks his way "amid these ruins." Jaspers also tries "to recover the Ariadne's thread that leads to the divine secrets." But his word on Kierkegaard is most moving:

50 *Le Mythe de Sisyphe* (Paris: Gallimard, 1942), p. 18.
51 Eugene Ionesco, "Dans les Armes de la Ville," Cahiers de la Compagnie Madeleine Fenaud—Jean-Louis Barrault, Paris, No. 20, October, 1957; quoted in Martin Esslin, *The Theater of the Absurd* (Garden City: Doubleday Anchor Books, 1961), p. xix.

> . . . Kierkegaard . . . does more than discover the absurd, he lives it. . . . Don Juan of the understanding, he multiplies pseudonyms and contradictions. . . . He refuses consolations, ethics, reliable principles. As for that thorn he feels in his heart, he is careful not to quit its pain. On the contrary, he awakens it and, in the desperate joy of a man crucified and happy to be so, he builds up piece by piece—lucidity, refusal, make-believe—a category of the man possessed. That face both tender and sneering, those pirouettes followed by a cry from the heart are the absurd spirit itself grappling with a reality beyond its comprehension. And the spiritual adventure that leads Kierkegaard to his beloved scandals begins likewise in the chaos of an experience divested of its setting and relegated to its original incoherence.[52]

Unfortunately Kierkegaard makes the absurd "the criterion of the other world, whereas it is simply a residue of the experience of this world."[53] He deifies the irrational. Hence the "leap" is an evasion. What is imperative is that we must turn away from subterfuge.

It was during this period of his work that Camus came up with Sisyphus as the Absurd hero. By reason of his scorn of the gods and his passion for life, the gods had condemned Sisyphus to roll a stone ceaselessly to the top of a mountain, only to have it roll down again of its own weight, renewing thereby the futile task wherein "the whole being is exerted toward accomplishing nothing. This is the price that must be paid for the passions of this earth." This is the representative anecdote of existentialist literature in its Sartrean phase. Man, says Sartre, "is a useless passion."

VI. THE LITERATURE OF
EXTREME SITUATIONS: SARTRE

But does it end here? This is the question we must ask of the literature of the Absurd.

---

[52] *The Myth of Sisyphus, and Other Essays*, trans. Justin OBrien (New York: Random House, 1961), p. 19.

[53] *Ibid.*, p. 28.

Sartre himself has attempted to translate his philosophical discourse into literary modes, on the theory that his phenomenological method confers upon the descriptive devices of literature as firm a claim to being "philosophy," if not a firmer claim, than may be held for formal discourse. His novels and his plays "describe" experience in existential and dramatic forms, whereas formal thinking, even when it "describes," deprives the data of their existential ubiquity.

In *The Flies* the Sartrean theses all appear: the hollowness of the gods, the struggle of the Self to assume the burden of its lonely but liberating freedom, the bad faith of those (of the city, of Electra) who would not, but who must protect themselves from reality by interposing gods, hierarchies, obediences, and conformity betwixt themselves and their own calls to responsible freedom. Orestes' dialogue with Zeus climaxes the argument with Orestes' affirmation of freedom ("I *am* my freedom"), with his assumption of his "exile" from "the fold," and with his acceptance of the responsibility involved—

> "The folk of Argos are my folk. I must open their eyes."
> "Poor people!" Zeus responds. ". . . What will they make of it?"
> "What they choose," Orestes replies. "They're free; and human life begins on the far side of despair."

This speech elicits from Zeus what is perhaps the pivotal statement of the play, so far as the Sartrean polemic goes. He replies:

> Well, Orestes, all this was foreknown. In the fullness of time a man was to come, to announce my decline. And you're that man, it seems.

This bold Christian theology on behalf of the Sartrean man is further enforced by Orestes' "coronation" and rejection by the people, his assumption of the "sins, remorse, night-fears, and the crime of Aegisthus" ("All are mine, I

take them all upon me"), and by his affirmation of his
kingdom ("All here is new, all must begin anew"). This
paraphrastic assumption of Christian Messianism would
seem to embody Sartre's proclamation of the new aeon and
the new man.

There is nothing quite comparable to this in the
Theater of the Absurd, unless it be found in Samuel
Beckett's *End Game,* where, at the end "of this game" which
the West has been playing, Hamm says of "God": "The
bastard! He doesn't exist!"; and Clov replies, "Not yet!"—
as though the authentic Christian gospel had been suppressed
or deflected or perverted by thought forms and practices
which took it captive, and prevented its coming to be. When
(in the French version) Clov looks out the window and
sees the little boy, we note in the dialogue which follows,
three allusions: one to the stone rolled away from Jesus'
tomb, one to Moses looking into the Promised Land, and
one to Buddha and the contemplative negative way—as
though the new way were perhaps appearing beyond the
parochialisms of any single religious vision. Through the
"naughting" of these the new may arise from an unforeseen
conjunction of their witnesses.

This is all the more startling when we compound the
several perspectives of the play: "End game" refers to the
late stages of a chess game; it may also be the "end phase"
in therapy; the time is Zero—a Cartesian charade; the action
takes place from within a skull—it begins with the self
waking; Hamm is a "God"-figure, born of our primitive
parentage (now in the ashcans), representing the middle
stage of human history from which a newer age may now—
with the demise of Hamm—emerge by way of a Vico-Joyce
cycle of the human story and its return upon itself. These
perspectives compound upon "the impending end," the
naughting of a Zero, and the "nothing [which is not yet]
is more real than [the] nothing" which is no more—to paraphrase Beckett's favorite quotation from Democritus.

Waiting for Godot, on the other hand, does not bring us so far, though it remains, perhaps, the more persistent image of the absurdity of the human condition—of its loneliness, of separateness in mutuality, of incommunicability, of the meaningless rigmarole of traditional theology. Lucky speaks of the divine apathy, aphasia (speechlessness), athambia (incapacity for terror or amazement), and of the disposition of the Divine to condemn people for reasons unknown. The play as a whole specifies our tendency to evade what we are, and to wait upon someone else (God? Godeau?) to carry the burden of our responsibilities. Meanwhile, "nothing happens, nobody comes, nobody goes, it's awful."

Sartre's *No Exit* contains a second theological disclosure, namely, that "Hell is—other people!" But its main concern is psychological, exhibiting the creeping stranglehold of destructive forces which three people in "bad faith" wreak upon one another as each attempts to impose his subjective aims upon the others.

More revealing, however, is Sartre's early novel, *La Nausée (Nausea)*, for it is here that the conflict of the Self with itself is set forth most compellingly. Antoine Roquentin, a French scholar and writer, begins to experience boredom, emptiness, panic, and fear. He encounters the absurdity of existence in the form of nausea, which sickness drives him upon existence as a disgusting and horrifying superfluity. He is an academician caught by the impertinence of tangibles—purple suspenders, the wall, the mirror, a broken chair, a pebble, and the imponderable root of a tree in the park. One thing abides—a jazz melody he had heard many times in a cafe, which mysteriously released him from his metaphysical anguish. This realization releases him also from his unconscious dependence upon the man whose life story he is researching; and, coming to terms with himself, he projects a book of his own, which shall be "beautiful and hard as steel and make people ashamed of their existence." Presumably *La Nausée* is that book.

Perhaps the most significant feature of this work is the descriptive detail of nausea which the author heaps upon the reader. One can scarcely avoid noting the anal erotism of Sartre's descriptive overtures. "I have it, the filth, the Nausea." "It spreads at the bottom of the viscous puddle, at the bottom of *our* time . . . ; it is made of wide, soft instants, spreading at the edge, like an oil stain . . . ." Existence, by way of the root in the park, had become "the very paste of things": the veneer of things "had melted, leaving soft, monstrous masses . . . ." "I hated this ignoble mess . . . filling everything with its gelatinous slither . . . . there was no *reason* for this flowing larva to exist . . . . And then suddenly the park emptied as through a great hole, the World disappeared as it had come . . . ."[54] It is a philosopher's picture of the world as excrescence and idea; or, since there is an unacknowledged mystical surd moving through Sartre's encounter with the Absurd, Sartre's hero moves (as does Daniel in *The Age of Reason*) through a dark "night of nausea" to find his "key to existence." It is in the scene in the park in *La Nausée* where Sartre's great refusal is made plain:

> I sank down on the bench, stupefied, stunned by this profusion of beings without origin; everywhere blossomings, hatchings out, my ears buzzed with existence, my very flesh throbbed and opened, abandoned itself to the universal burgeoning. It was repugnant.[55]

This is indicative of Sartre's failure to grasp the dimension of the Absurd as an ab-surd, as Camus and Ionesco have been able in different ways to do. With Sartre the primary wonder of things is vitiated by a stubborn scabrous and scatological seriousness which pervades his work and diminishes it. He is without humor, as he is without pathos. He has wit, but his wit does not reach the unconscious, hence it functions as rhetoric of polemic instead of poetic

---

[54] *Nausea*, (Norfolk, Conn.: New Directions, 1959), pp. 29, 33, 171, 172, 180, 181.

[55] *Ibid.*, pp. 178–179.

conceit. His antirationalism remains rationalist; his anti-bourgeois actionism remains bourgeois. His turn to art (as we have seen above) becomes "a summons by one freedom to another," and so becomes "committed," "engaged," as putting oneself "in every instance in the position of condemning violence from the point of view of the members of the oppressed classes."[56] But such an attitude, as Ionesco was not slow to point out, "leads directly to the concentration camp."[57] Aesthetically, the temptation is toward art as propaganda, or journalese (as in *The Reprieve* or *The Mandarins* of Simone de Beauvoir) .

VII. THE LITERATURE OF
EXTREME SITUATIONS: CAMUS

There are three ways out of this pride and petulance of doctrinaire aggressiveness: the ways of Camus, Ionesco, and Rilke—of pathos, comedy, and poetry. The Theater of the Absurd is already beyond it. It no longer rolls the stones of Sisyphus. Camus alone adheres to his own anecdote and breaks free from within it.

He achieves this release in two ways. In the first place he does not refuse the mystical surd implicit in the encounter with the Absurd; in the second, he permits the ironic transmutation of the Sisyphus anecdote into the pathos of the Christian parable as a more adequate account of the irony of the human situation. It does not matter that he extracts from Christian parable its irony; it suffices that his quest for the representative anecdote moves into it.

---

[56] "The Responsibility of the Writer" (a lecture presented at the Sorbonne in Paris on the occasion of the first general meeting of UNESCO, November 1, 1946), reprinted in *The Creative Vision, Modern European Writers on Their Art,* ed. Block and Salinger (New York: Grove Press, 1960), pp. 173, 185.

[57] Lerminier, "Dialogue avec Ionesco," p. 53; quoted in Richard N. Coe: *Eugene Ionesco* (New York: Grove Press, 1961), p. 85.

First, however, comes his acceptance of life:

> . . . if there is a sin against life, it consists perhaps not so much in despairing of life as in hoping for another life and in eluding the implacable grandeur of this life.[58]

Again, in "Return to Tipasa," he speaks of "another mysterious voice, within me" through which he learns that "the secret I am seeking lies hidden in a valley full of olive trees." It is Mersault's discovery (in *L'Étrangère* [*The Stranger*], Camus's first novel) : when "gazing up at the dark sky spangled with its signs and stars, for the first time, the first, I laid my heart open to the benign indifference of the universe." This confession significantly parallels Camus's statement in *L'Homme Révolté* (*The Rebel*): "One can reject all history and yet accept the world of the sea and the stars."[59] But the most striking of all is the allusion in *The Myth of Sisyphus* itself to the moment of "the rock's victory." Here he remarks, "these are our nights of Gethsemane," and—a page later—he speaks of the "unconscious, secret calls" which teach us the peculiar victory, that "there is no sun without shadow, and it is essential to know the night. The absurd man says yes and his effort will henceforth be unceasing."[60] I have commented elsewhere on Camus's "dark night of the Absurd,"[61] but we must at least note here that, whereas Kierkegaard's dialectic carried him into his "Night of the Absolute," Camus's pathos leads him to the night of Gethsemane.

La Chute (*The Fall*) confirms this in its reinstatement

---

[58] "Summer in Algiers," included in the American edition of *The Myth of Sisyphus*, p. 113.

[59] *The Stranger*, trans. Stuart Gilbert (New York: Alfred A. Knopf, 1946), p. 154; *The Rebel*, trans. Anthony Bower (New York: Alfred A. Knopf, 1956), p. 276.

[60] *The Myth of Sisyphus, op. cit.*, pp. 90, 91.

[61] *Christian Faith and the Contemporary Arts*, ed. Finley Eversole (Nashville: Abingdon Press, 1962), "Camus: The Argument from the Absurd," pp. 124ff.

of the Christian parable by its inversion of ironic paraphrase. It features *le recit,* the monologue of Jean-Baptiste Clamence, an inverted *vox clamantis in deserto*—a prophet for empty times, an Elijah without a Messiah, crying in the wilderness of the Absurd. For it was this which overtook Clamence when his life—the role-playing of his self-esteem —was shattered by the cry upon the bridge. A woman jumped into the Seine, and he—did nothing. Shortly after, he heard the mysterious laugh which followed him thereafter and drove him into his vocation as the "judge-penitent" who, through confessing his failure to strangers whom he encounters, holds up to them the mirror of defection, our universal sham, the persistent fall of all pretensions into alienation, duplicity, and compounding guilt. Clamence becomes the Apostle of the Laugh[62]—by proclaiming "the melancholy of the common condition and the despair of not being able to escape it."

This common condition is "the fall" (*La Chute*); but, despite the persistent paraphrase of Christian doctrines, it is not the Fall in the Christian sense. Despite the references to Eden (from which he fell), to the burning bush, to the Sadducees, to the Scriptures, to the concentric canals of Amsterdam as the circles of hell (themselves being in the last circle, the circle of the treacherous and the misbelievers), to his own name of Jean-Baptiste, to judgment, to Dante's limbo of ambivalent neutrality, to the font of holy water, to the Last Judgment ("it takes place every day"), to the crucifixion, to Peter, to the paraphrase of Christ as the mirror which shows man to himself—despite all this, the Christian sense is not decisive. The Fall is a falling away of the self from itself—from its potentiality for being itself, in the Heideggerian sense. It is a falling away into inauthenticity, into the puddle of everydayness, into the crowd, and

---

[62] Cf. Hazel E. Barnes, *The Literature of Possibility, A Study in Humanistic Existentialism* (Lincoln: University of Nebraska Press, 1959), p. 146.

into groundlessness. It is what Sartre would call "bad faith";
but Camus's exploitation of the factors of ambiguity, duplicity, talkativeness, alienation and lassitude bring this entan-
glement of the Self within itself into Heidegger's vision of
the downward plunge "into the groundlessness and nullity
of inauthentic everydayness" whereby the self-understanding
is always torn away from authenticity ("though always with
a sham of authenticity").[63]

What, then, is the outcome, the irony of this irony?
He has petitioned the Christian postulates, though not in a
Christian way. *Nevertheless he has petitioned them,* and so
reinstated them, albeit ironically, and in the context of our
falling away from authenticity. He has kept the wound of the
negative open. But in our inauthentic betrayals of ourselves,
we swarm like judges upon the innocents: the followers of
Christ and those of the Antichrist are just the same, equally
judgmental, equally sham. "Yes, we have lost the track of
the light, the mornings, the holy innocence of those who
forgive themselves." So, in the negative dynamisms of our
pooled inauthenticities we crucify (and are crucified by)
one another (we are "all Christs in our mean manner").
What is essential is that we should risk our lives for authenticity. "Please tell me what happened to you one night on
the quays of the Seine and how you managed never to risk
your life." But this is not Sisyphus rolling the stone. The
anecdote has changed. We have been forced upon and
through the night of Gethsemane, and upon another man
carrying another burden up another hill. (It will be useful
to recall at this point the passage from Kierkegaard's
Training in Christianity quoted above (p. 111), in which
Christ as paradigm, as mirror, as contradiction, is adduced.
This passage might well have been the original, the source,

---

[63] Martin Heidegger, *Being and Time*, trans. John Macquarrie and Ed-
ward Robinson (London: SCM Press, 1962), Section 38, pp. 219ff.

of Camus's parable. ("While he is judging, what dwells within him must be revealed.")

VIII. THE LITERATURE OF THE ABSURD

Now it is quite possible that the author of *The Fall* was one of those whom Kierkegaard described as privately having a rendezvous with the Deity, for it was Kierkegaard's view that as soon as the uncertainty of all things "has been thought infinitely," the Deity will be present. This, however, is just what is not clear—at least not in Camus. He has taken us most adroitly in the net of his designing. We are convicted, but curiously not appeased. We remain stuck fast in the irony, successfully duped by Jean-Baptiste Clamence. To be sure we have moved beyond the negative vision of Sartre and into the *Verfallen* of Heidegger. Yet we do not move into "the open" as Heidegger's vision invites us to do. Perhaps Camus's pathos remains a pathos of irony rather than a pathos of the Absurd? When the Absurd "has been thought infinitely," should it not empty into the pathos of comedy—and so into "the open"? It is a difficult line to draw.

In the work of Jean Genet, for example, we begin with a Sartrean premise: our persistence in role-playing. This mystery of role-playing is central to *The Maids,* and to *The Balcony,* and to *The Blacks.* But other dimensions are added. Ritual patterns are introduced and played as a game in an inverted religious solemnity, which returns upon itself in a repetition of its magical appeal. A dream dimension is added, and the ritual is further distanced from reality to become a ritual of wish-fulfillment. In *The Blacks* one bank of Negro actors ("blacks") is reflected by another bank of blacks attired and masked as "whites," and the ritual sacrifice is played to mask an action off-stage ("outside"), which is itself a play within a play. In *The Balcony* men and women play their roles in Madame Irma's brothel (a metaphor of our world). They are surrounded by mirrors which reflect the role upon the role-player, compounding the blur of line and definition between reality and illusion, dream and appearance. It is a game of mirrors, in which man is trapped in a reduplicating recession of his own images, leading off into being's absurd negation of itself. "In this pyramid of fantasies," writes Sartre, "the ultimate appearance derealizes all others."[64] The characters become "metaphors of what they represent." Still more basically, "in these patient fakings, appearance is revealed at the same time as pure nothingness and as cause of itself."[65] Thus not only is the problem of self-identity posed, and the problem of reality versus illusion, but being itself drops away into the recessive naughtings of its own projections and reflections, and the myth of Sisyphus is exchanged for the circular sophistry of Epimenides: "Epimenides says that Cretans are liars. But he is a Cretan. Therefore he lies. Therefore Cretans are not liars. Therefore, he speaks the truth, etc., etc." "Truth leads to the lie and vice-versa."[66]

There is one point, however, where the circularity may be broken. This occurs in *The Balcony*. The people here show a passion for having their roles verified through acceptance by others. This becomes possible through the "nomenclature." Who controls the nomenclature controls the state! The nomenclature establishes the order of things and the hierarchy of meanings. It founds the language. It is the framework created by ourselves or accepted from the hands of our forebears; it is a symbolic world imposed upon the evanescent phantasmagoria of appearances. At this point, Genet has moved into the sphere of Heidegger's later think-

---

[64] Jean-Paul Sartre, introduction to *The Maids* and *Deathwatch*, (New York: Grove Press, 1954),pp. 30f.

[65] *Ibid.*, p. 31.

[66] *Ibid.*, p. 7.

ing; but the affirmation is no sooner given than it is withdrawn—the nomenclature is as brittle, or as insubstantial, as
the "storehouse of mummery" (and memory!) which sus-
tains it.

When we turn to Ionesco, we plunge beyond this. The
Absurd is "thought infinitely." It empties into hilarity and
we are in the Aristophanic-Heraclitean world. Mushrooms
blossom, corpses grow, furniture, chairs, eggs, cups prolif-
erate, men contract rhinoceritis and a splendor of pachy-
derms thunders across the body politic (as monstrosity
displaced humanity in the Second World War). The
premises are existential, even Sartrean. When recollecting
a childhood scene, Ionesco remarks:

> . . . everything strikes me indeed as shadow and evanescence.
> I am seized with dizziness, with anguish. There, in effect, goes the
> world: a desert of flying shadows.[67]

Two fundamental "states of consciousness" are at the
basis of his plays: evanescence and heaviness, emptiness and
superfluous presence, transparency and opaqueness, light
and heavy shadow. All is contradiction and infinite coincidence. The "sweet, imprisoning security" of the causal cos-
mos of Aristotelian reason is abandoned for a universe of
limitless and incomprehensible absurdity. Language, founded
on those classical pinions, cripples in mid-flight and falls
with unheroic thud upon our platitudes, or plunges into
voids of meaninglessness:

> . . . all reality, all language seems to become disjointed, to
> fall apart, to empty itself of meaning, so that, since all is devoid
> of importance, what else can one do but laugh at it?[68]

This crack-up of language—founded upon the rationalistic
fallacy which supposes that meaning derived from the ex-

67 "Qu'est-ce que l'avant-garde en 1958," p. 1; quoted in Richard N.
68 "Point de Depart," p. 18; quoted in Coe, *op. cit.*, p. 63.
Coe: *Eugene Ionesco* (New York: Grove Press, 1961), p. 71.

perience can be prepacked abstractly and conceptually—is symbolic of the emptying of all of our conventions in Western culture so founded and so coerced: they have become "hollow within and encrusted without, and in consequence, elementally *stupid*—and elementally *comic*."[69]

There are obvious points of rapport with the Sartrean vision here; but we move radically beyond it at three points. The theater, for Ionesco, serves no utilitarian purpose; it aims not at *engagement* but at *degagement*—though Ionesco holds paradoxically that this disengagement is "a usefulness without which we cannot live." Second, there is an appeal here from *rationalist* "lucidity" to the *fantastic* lucidities of our subjective life—dream, nightmare, fantasy, imagination. ("What is objectivity, if not a consensus of different subjectivities?") "Fantasy is revealing; it is a method of cognition: everything that is imagined is true; nothing is true if it is not imagined."[70] As against Kierkegaard (see p. 116 above) imagination and fantasy come *before* the dialectic, not after, and retain therefore Kierkegaard's prized "immediacy." Thus humor and comedy become possible and literary forms are not confined to those of wit and dialectic. But finally, and this is all-important, the comic vision somersaults from "nausea" into wonder. The lucid perception of meaninglessness becomes the one thing full of meaning. The Absurd contains its own reversal. "To attack the absurdity (of the human condition) is a way of stating the possibility of non-absurdity."[71] The comic is itself the pure intuition of the Absurd; it effects that detachment which is beyond both hope and despair. It brings us by the surprise of joy into what Heidegger calls "the clearing," and we are delivered by laughter's liberation into serenity and awe. "The

[69] *Ibid.*, p. 47.

[70] "La Demystification par l'Humour Noir," *L'Avant-Scene*, February 15, 1959; quoted in Esslin, *op. cit.*, p. 130.

[71] Quoted in Esslin, *op. cit.*, p. 138.

astonishment of being invades me." Quite unexpectedly we
have come upon that "narrow escape into faith" which
Christopher Fry has ascribed to comedy's artifice—"even
though knowledge of the cause is always twitched away from
us."[72]

We must note with some care, however, what has
happened here. These metaphors of the human condition
contrived by the Theater of the Absurd "to cause the mask
to fall" (Artaud) and lead men into seeing themselves as
they really are, are really pugnacious charades and riddles,
enigmas, conundrums, "cosmogonic teasers" (Huizinga),
teasing us out of time into deformity, drawing us through
the facades and scenarios of our screens of "knowing" upon
the raw abysm and perplexity of things. Beckett's charade
of two men on an empty open road, exploring nullity,
"evading what one cannot evade, . . . evading what one is"
(Sartre); Ionesco's detective-psychoanalyst stuffing bread into
the throat of Choubert (in *Victims of Duty*) to stop up the
"hole in being" (Sartre) when he descends into his subconscious; Pinter's two gunmen striving desperately to send
"two sago puddings" via a dumbwaiter to the powers above;
Adamov's dramatic saga of two men (in *Le Ping-Pong*)
devoting their lives to a pinball machine—a symbol of our
human objectives generally—and ending, as old men, futilely
playing ping-pong: these are all charades and parables of
the human situation. We have returned to the precincts
of religion, and to the origins of philosophy.

According to Heraclitus, "Nature and life are a *griphos*,
an enigma," a riddle, and man himself is "the riddle-solver."
"Nature (*phusis*) loves to hide herself" (Fr. 123). The
ritual riddle contest, which appears in all the great religions,
brings us into the realm of sacred play, from which it is but
a step to festive play and martial play, to disputation and the

play of wit and mimicry.[73] Philosophically, it may take a Socratic form, as when Plato suggests (in *Symposium*, 223D) that the authentic poet should be comic and tragic at once, or Socrates remarks (in *Cratylus*, 440): "For the appearance and names of these gods there is a humorous as well as a serious explanation, for the gods are fond of a joke." The Castle's messengers told K. that he was too serious and couldn't understand a joke (see p. 108 above).

But Kierkegaard saw even more clearly how closely the comic abuts upon the religious. For him the humorist places the God-idea "in conjunction with other things and evokes the contradiction—but he does not maintain a relationship to God in terms of religious passion *stricte sic dictus,* he transforms himself instead into a jesting and yet profound exchange-center for all these transactions, but he does not himself stand related to God."[74] But when God or the gods have withdrawn, and there are no gods to be fond of the humorist's joke, or no God for whom he can serve as exchange-center for these godly transactions, then the comic riddle, like Rilke's sphinx, thrusts "the human face on the scale of the stars" (*Duino Elegies*, X).

The humorist also reads the ciphers of his own transcendence. But the ultimate cipher is now existence itself; and man once made "in the image of God" is man in search of his image. It is a strange situation. The return to our primordial striving should herald the approach of the hero, with his tasks to perform, his trials to overcome, his ordeals to pass through, his obstacles to surmount, his dragons to slay. He should come incognito, his identity hidden, wearing a mask, in disguise, and carrying a secret. "Once more we are close to the old and sacred game of the hidden being

---

[73] See Johann Huizinga, *Homo Ludens, A Study of the Play-Element in Culture* (Boston: Beacon Press, 1950, 1960), pp. 116ff.; cf. also Werner Jaeger, *Paideia,* I (New York: Oxford University Press, 1945), pp. 180–181.

[74] *Concluding Unscientific Postscript*, p. 451.

who will only reveal himself to the initiated."[75] It would appear that the hero quest is today transformed. It is a journey of inwardness. It is a desperate journey. It is the "vision and enigma" of Zarathustra:

> Condemned of thyself, and to thine own stoning: O Zarathustra, far indeed threwest thou thy stone—but upon *thyself* will it recoil! . . .
>
> Courage slayeth also giddiness at abysses: and where doth man not stand at abysses! Is not seeing itself—seeing abysses? . . .
>
> Ye daring ones around me! Ye venturers. . . . Ye enigma-enjoyers!
>
> . . . *what* did I then behold in parable?
>
> *Who* is the shepherd into whose throat the serpent thus crawled? . . .
>
> The shepherd however bit as my cry had admonished him. . . . Far away did he spit the head of the serpent . . .; and sprang up. . . .
>
> No longer shepherd, no longer man—a transfigured being, a light-surrounded being, that *laughed!*[76]

IX. THE HEIDEGGERIAN PERSPECTIVE

Thus we arrive at the third and concluding phase—the Heideggerian phase of our study. Instead of Job, or Sisyphus, as the representative anecdote, we come upon Zarathustra;

---

[75] Huizinga, *op. cit.*, p. 133. It is important to note again how perceptive Kierkegaard was vis-à-vis such perspectives as these. Having dropped substantialistic Christologies along with Intellectualism in theology, he twice qualifies his image of Christ as the *mirror* which shows man to himself. Christ is also the *riddle* which reveals what is within a man by how he guesses—an infinite risk. At the same time, he is an *incognito*: "The form of a servant means unrecognizableness.— . . . absolute unrecognizableness . . . the greatest possible . . . remove from being God, and therefore the profoundest incognito." *Training in Christianity*, pp. 126–127. Compare also Camus's *Jean-Baptiste Clamence* as an incognito of the *vox clamantis in deserto* and Kierkegaard's *Johannes de Silentio*.

[76] Friedrich Nietzsche, *Thus Spake Zarathustra*, trans. Thomas Common (New York: Modern Library, n.d.), pp. 172–176.

instead of the maieutic of Socrates, or the reason-will dialectic of the Stoics, we come upon Heraclitus; instead of Pascal, or Descartes, we come upon Nietzsche. But what is most admirable here is that the anecdote of Zarathustra is seeking a deeper and profounder form; the Socratic-rationalist dialectic is moving toward the pre-Socratic recognition of the primal mystery of the Logos; and the Nietzschean clamor is yielding to the poetry of Hölderlin and Rainer Maria Rilke.

All is here transformed. Instead of the metaphors of nausea, the hole, viscosity, the stare, *engagement,* etc., we encounter "care," "befalling," "building," "sojourning," "dwelling," "the open," "homecoming," "releasement" (*Gelassenheit*), "Logos." Poetry returns. Who does not live either poetically or religiously is a fool, asserted Kierkegaard; but here the either/or of the dualistic dissonance drops away. Rather we begin: "Poetically man dwells upon the earth" (Hölderlin). According to Sartre, existentialism "is nothing else than an attempt to draw all the consequences of a coherent atheistic position";[77] but this is not what Heidegger says. The terms "atheistic" and "theistic" belong to another universe of discourse. Ours is "the time of the gods that have fled *and* of the god that is coming. It is the time *of need,* because it lies under a double lack and a double Not: the No-more of the gods that have fled and the Not-yet of the god that is coming."[78]

The self, for Kierkegaard, must relate itself to itself by relating itself to the power that posited it; but here the self relates to the logos of Being—the Being that is beyond our knowing save through the mythos of our naming. The self, for Sartre, is always a project of the for-itself in transcension of the in-itself; for Heidegger, man is a shepherd of

77 Jean-Paul Sartre, *Existentialism* (is a Humanism), pp. 60–61.

78 Martin Heidegger, "Hölderlin and the Essence of Poetry," in *Existence and Being, ed.,* with an introduction, by Werner Brock (London: Vision Press, 1949), p. 313.

Being, who, by his response to the call of Being, actively brings Being into openness and guards it in his sayings. Instead of a "hole in being" we find an open place, "a clearing," an "elucidating center" by whose fire (Heraclitus)—"the sway held by light"—things are made to shine (*scheinen*) and thus are made to appear (*erscheinen*). The truth (*aletheia*) consists in this unconcealment of Being coming into appearance through things. Thus the primordial strife (Heraclitus) of truth is ever between hiddenness and elucidation, just as in existence it is between earth as given and world as assembled about the opening Word. It is here that the art work and the work of the poet appear.

In poetry and the work of art we behold the hiddenness of Being arising into unhiddenness. It is this disclosure which is the task of the poet and of which he is the guardian and on behalf of which he takes his risk—of guessing the riddle, of naming the gods. Thus poetry, which is not characteristic of the Kierkegaardian existentialism, and is almost wholly absent from the Sartrean world, is of the very essence of the Heideggerian vision.

The importance of this view for literature can hardly be overstated. It is a recognition, by way of a "fundamental ontology," of the fact that all language is at bottom metaphorical and all meaning moves between "earth" and "Logos" by way of the "Mythos" of world-building or the play of our *figurae* (*Weltspiel*). Implicit in this are three far-reaching judgments having to do with (*a*) the nature of language, (*b*) literature as poetry, and (implicit but as yet unrecognized in Heidegger) (*c*) the rediscovery of the literature of quest.

Concerning the problem of language it should be noted that *all* of the existentialists, including the "drama of non-communication" (Beckett, Ionesco, *et al.*), have focused upon this problem. "Man is a twaddler," wrote Kierkegaard, "— and that with the help of speech." We surprise him here, no doubt, basking a little in the ricochets of his own brilliance; but the *Journal* entry (Dru, #1383) is entitled "Man," and he goes on to say that "with the help of speech every man participates in the highest"; but unhappily we succumb to participation in the highest with the help of speech "by talking nonsense about it, [which] is just as ironical as to participate in a royal banquet as a spectator from the gallery." Hence the "dialectical deceit," the enervation, the "talkativeness," the anonymity of the present age in which and through which our meanings are progressively emptied and everyone turns to the things "outside."[79]

Sartre's view of language does not help as much. He is aware of its "sickness" today;[80] but language is not healed in his philosophy: it merely becomes an instrument in the service of a philosophy of action. Language "arises" in us as a result of our encounters with the Other. The Other's "look" destroys my subjectivity and reduces me to the status of an object.[81] Out of this situation the primal conflict arises. Language is in the service of this conflict. It is at once defensive and aggressive, a means for conquest over others (as in Sartre's analogies with the body and with love), yet frustrated always by reason of the other's objectivizations of me. So far as Parain's "word-sickness" goes, Sartre falls back upon Kant's synthetic propositions and upon the Cartesian *cogito* in such wise that the familiar subject-object split emerges again and absconds with the existentialist marbles—the radical question of a truth for man that is more than a "truth" of reason.

Sartre's play, *Kean*, might be taken as an admirable presentation of the self's encounter with the other in all its aspects of defense and aggression; but it is even more devastating in its exploitation of the role-player's search for identity

[79] Cf. *The Present Age*, trans. Dru and Lowrie (New York: Oxford University Press, 1940), p. 15 *et passim*.

[80] Cf. Sartre's essay on Brice Parain, "The Journey and Return," in *Essays on Language and Literature*, ed. J. L. Hevesi (London: Allen Wingate, 1947), pp. 143ff.

[81] Jean-Paul Sartre, *Being and Nothingness*, pp. 372–375.

through the complex masquerades of the play within the play (the role within the role). It presents a comedy of cancellations toward nullity induced by reflections encountering reflections in the rationalist's hall of mirrors.

Heidegger seeks a return to the Source. He would go behind Kant and Descartes, Aristotle and Plato, to the primary question (as posed by the pre-Socratic thinkers) of Being itself, as to why *anything at all is*. Existence is that which stands out (ec-sistance) in Being. It is the irony of "humanistic" existentialism that man's thought recoils upon man thinking and reinstates the problem it had thought to overcome. Language for Heidegger is "the house of Being." When this is forgotten, the ego becomes a center projecting its own goals and manipulating (using) *things* and others to achieve its ends. Thus all is reduced to the realm of objects. Language itself becomes a tool. It becomes "chatter" as its mystery is degraded, and its source in the Logos forgotten; thence it enters necessarily into the complicities of our falling (*Verfallen*) away from Being. Kierkegaard's "twaddle" and Heidegger's "chatter" are, at bottom, the same; yet it is not without interest that the word "chatter" is *charrada* in provincial French—the source of our word "charade." Through language and gesture we play out the charades of our "knowing." Yet when the great Riddle of Being is not acknowledged, when the Ciphers of Transcendence are no longer read (Jaspers), we play at riddles as a form of idleness, and language becomes a block to renewal. To remove the block to being the language must be reminted. It must renew its relation to Logos. Which is the task and risk of the poet. Like the shepherd he must go out into the open. (Poetry "is the most innocent of occupations"—almost like a game: but it is a risky game—"language is the most dangerous of possessions"; for with it the poet must name the gods.) The poet is the shepherd of being.[82]

---

82 Martin Heidegger, *Platons Lehre von der Wahrheit*, (Bern: Verlag A. Francke Ag., 1947), pp. 75, 90.

X. HOLDERLIN, RILKE, AND THE ORPHEUS JOURNEY

One of the most pertinent recognitions of this guardianship will be found in Rilke's lines of the 10th of August, 1926 (the source of Heidegger's insight?), when, in describing those who are set apart "to attain the purest," he writes:

> They must stand like the shepherd, outlasting,
> from afar it may seem that he mourns,
> coming nearer one feels how he watches.

This "watching" in our time is radical. Both Hölderlin and Rilke were profoundly aware of the fact that our gods are withdrawn. It is the poet who must go, in this knowledge and under these circumstances, into "the open" and there, with patience, await "the new name of God." It is a dangerous encounter with Being, as Hölderlin well knew:

> Yet it behoves us, under the storms of God,
> Ye poets! with uncovered head to stand,
> With our own hand to grasp the very lightning flash
> Paternal, and to pass, wrapped in song,
> The divine gift to the people.[83]

Heidegger accepts this view, seeing in it a "return to the Source." It is through this act that the language is founded and "the High One" named. "Only and for the first time in this Between is it decided, who man is and where he is settling his existence."[84]

When Heidegger turns to Hölderlin and Rilke, he sees the poet undertaking such a task. Hölderlin saw the decline of our culture into its twilight (*der Abend der Weltzeit*) with

---

[83] *Wie wenn am Feiertage.*

[84] "Hölderlin and the Essence of Poetry," *op. cit.*, p. 312. I have treated this theme more extensively in my essay on "The Naming of the Gods in Hölderlin and Rilke" in *Christianity and the Existentialists*, ed. Carl Michalson (New York: Charles Scribner's Sons, 1956).

the dropping away of the "unique three"—Hercules, Dionysus, and Christ. Rilke is the poet who seeks, through song, to
rediscover the lost spoor of the gods. Heidegger elicits from
Rilke's poetry a series of axial terms: "Nature," "Risk," the
"Open," the "pure Relation," "Being," "the Sayable," "Presence," and "Song." Certain other terms—"dwelling," "sojourning," "homecoming," "festivity," and the like—come
clearly from Hölderlin. These terms continue to function in
the later work of Heidegger. They comprise a series of point-
ers to the movement and deeper meaning of his work.

Most significant of all may be his recognition of the
place of "Song" in Rilke's poetry and its bearing upon the
poet's aspiration to live out of his "pure relation" to Being.
For Rilke *Gesang ist Dasein*—Song *is* existence (*Sonnets to
Orpheus,* i, 3)—which may be easy for the god, but (asks
Rilke) when do *we* exist? When does the god spend the earth
and stars upon *our* being? Rilke answers that it is not in the
loving and singing of youth or in youth's "sudden song."
Forget it, he says. It will not endure. We must live our way
into a singing in the truth in which, lyre-wise, the god
breathes through us, and we become in pure openness the
music of Being's exhalation through this finite but songful
occasion. This is the ec-stasis of *Dasein.* "Song is the hearing," says Heidegger, "in the wholeness of the pure relation."[85] It results from that superabounding existence
springing up in the heart to which Rilke refers in the last
line of his Ninth Elegy, and which Heidegger compares
with Pascal's reasons of the heart which reason knows not
of.[86] It might also be related to Heraclitus' "ever-living, self-
kindling fire."[87]

85 Martin Heidegger, *Holzwege* (Frankfurt: Vittorio Klostermann, 1950),
p. 293.

86 *Ibid.,* p. 282. Rilke's line reads: "Uberzahliges Dasein/entspringt mir
im Herzen" ("Supernumerous existence springs up in my heart").

87 Fragment #29. Philip Wheelright, *Heraclitus* (Princeton: Princeton
University Press, 1959), p. 37.

What Heidegger curiously fails to develop is that the encounter with the gods, both for Hölderlin and for Rilke, is a journey—not just any journey, but a journey of a particular kind. Yet he seems intuitively aware of it. Hölderlin's hymn, entitled "Voyage," is "full of riddles." It contains a journey "to the Source" and a return. But, writes Heidegger:

> . . . such a return is only possible for one who has previously, and perhaps for a long time now, borne on his shoulders as the wanderer the burden of the voyage, and has gone over into the source, so that he could there experience what the nature of the Sought-For might be, and then be able to come back more experienced, as the Seeker. "That which thou seekest is near, and already coming to meet thee."[88]

This is excellent and underscores the central paradox contained in Hölderlin's lines. But the inwardness of this journey is not specified, though it is common to Hölderlin, Nietzsche, and Rilke. Alienation from reality, revealed in Hölderlin's hymn, inducing the retrospective longing, the longing to return to the maternal depths where he might "like the sleeping nursling, breathe the Heavenly ones" is the libidinal temptation to withdraw from reality—though it may well be the way of the hero in these times. Following the descent the "sun journey" (note Hölderlin's desperate appeal to Apollo) should begin. The poet who would name the gods (as well as exhibit our condition) must not only journey *into* the depth, but must return.[89]

Rilke's appeal to Orpheus is therefore significant. For it is Orpheus, whose power of song would permit him to commute between the upper and nether worlds, who can sing praises "among shadows too," who teaches us how "to dance

[88] "Remembrance of the Poet," Brock, *op. cit.*, p. 279.

[89] Heidegger's treatment of these poems should be compared on this point with that of Carl G. Jung, in his *Psychology of the Unconscious* (New York: Dodd, Mead & Co., 1952), pp. 435ff.

the orange," to bring to earth its "invisible re-arising in us," who "pours himself out as a spring," and who makes us aware that "only song over the land hallows and celebrates."

At one point Heidegger glimpses this dimension. He notes with approval Rilke's reference (in his letter to Nora Purtscher-Wydenbruck, August 11, 1924) to "the depth dimension of our inner being" in which Rilke recognizes the place and function of the unconscious. This is not for Rilke an escape from things: it is the source to be lived from. His search for the "pure Relation" implies this recognition. When he casts it in religious terms, it is the same. Instead of "looking at" God, as we have habitually done (thus converting Him into an object, and so placing Him over against us with all that this implies), should we not try "to see as God sees"—in which case God would be "behind us," as it were: we would not be facing Him, but looking away from Him, looking in the direction in which He is looking. Then we should see all things as He sees them. We should be released from the idolatrous stance of objectivizing doctrine. In Heideggerian terms, we should be living from the Source, or from Being. Being would stand out (ec-sist) in us. We would learn to let things be, in the integrity of their being. In mythological terms, we should be resuming the Chthonic-Dionysian element in experiencing ourselves in relation to reality. Thus it is not Zarathustra, but Orpheus, who has become the representative anecdote of existentialism in its third, and most significant, phase.

XI. DELMORE SCHWARTZ AND THE HERACLITEAN RIDDLE

The Apollonian delinquency of the Western consciousness has been sharply etched in a poem by Delmore Schwartz, whose own journey has led him through all the phases of the existentialist revolt—in its philosophical, aesthetic, and psychological modes: through Pascal, Kierkegaard, Kafka's point of no return, into the Sartrean (but, in Schwartz's case, Whiteheadian) "withness of the body," and beyond these into the Heideggerian-Heraclitean transformation of "water into wine at each marriage in Cana of Galilee"—into that world of metaphorical astonishment in which poetry "is quick as tigers, clever as cats, vivid as oranges" and "the actuality of possibility."

> Once, when I was a boy,
> Apollo summoned me
> To be apprenticed to the endless summer of light and consciousness,
> And thus to become and be what poets often have been,
> A shepherd of being, a riding master of being, holding the sun-god's horses, leading his sheep, training his eagles,
> Directing the constellations to their stations, and to each grace of place.

But there came a time when the great-god called, and he followed Dionysus, forgetting Apollo. Yet in this, he discovered, he was wrong—to suppose that one cannot serve *both* gods. For it is through the uniting of the two (Orpheus descending and ascending) that disaster, tragedy, mistake may always become "a fabulous discovery of America, of the opulence hidden in the dark depths and glittering heights of reality."[90] What is quite marvelous in Schwartz's work is the way in which he compounds *two* journeys, those of Orpheus *and* Abraham, and thus resumes the ethical integrity of the Kierkegaardian existentialism with the ontological opulence of Heidegger's: "Abraham and Orpheus, be with me now

> . . . you . . . who lifted up the knife,
> And you, musician in the after-life. . . .

Then—in his later poetry—these journeys become one moment, a continuing moment perpetually renewed: the mo-

[90] Schwartz, "Once and for All," in *Summer Knowledge* (Garden City: Doubleday & Co., 1959), p. 222.

ment of the phoenix, symbol of resurrection and rebirth, archetype of all the transformations:

> By thinking of how all arise and aspire to the nature of fire, to the flame-like climbing of vine and leaf and flower,
> And calling to mind how all things must suffer and die in growth and birth,
> To be reborn, again and again and again, to be transformed all over again.
> The desire of the bud and the flower and the fruit of the tree and the vine to be devoured and to be phoenix in nature, fulfilled in the phoenix sensuality of blood and of wine, or stilled in the mud near the root under the ground once more awaiting the sun's domination, the sun's great roar and fire.[91]

This is, of course, a Heraclitean vision, a bit too knowing perhaps, but letting the *griphos* be, riddling still behind the appearances. As Hölderlin put it,

> A riddle is a pure leap into being. Even
> Song is hardly allowed to unveil it.

Which is to say that all creativity arises in plenitude from secret and hidden sources, the god playing behind the veil, bestowing in grace and place its gifts and surprises, around which we assemble our words and our worlds of meaning.

> ... How could it be otherwise? For truth abides
> Hidden in the future, in the ambush of the marvellous,
> Unknown and monstrous, at the very heart of surprise.[92]

Existentialism may be seen, then, as revealed by the literature which appears under its sign, as a surprising *élan* toward radical renewal. It cuts behind the rationalist pretensions of the self-sufficient ego, which has itself emptied our culture's symbols of their mytho-poetic powers, and delivered its own "logic" into the Absurd. Theology also, if it persists in piling a divinity on top of these logical systems, by what-

---

[91]"May's Truth and May's Falsehood," in *Summer Knowledge*, p. 214.
[92]"Jacob," in *Summer Knowledge*, p. 233.

ever artifice of conceptualist analogy, only compounds the dilemma by making an alliance with "God." Theology too must risk its radical recasting. When the symbols are emptied and no longer elicit the response of those who would dwell under them, a period has ended. The symbol structures fall. In the absurd clutter and rubble about us, we are thrown back upon ourselves to relate our supposed *personae* once more to the depth within and the unencompassable without. Just as the literature of existentialism probes into the roots of the Unconscious, making thereby an inevitable alliance with the psychologies of depth, so also it unveils "the Holy" by a succession of unforeseen recognitions.

The somewhat strident either/or of Kierkegaard lapses through keeping the wound of the negative open. It lapses by way of the absurd into our cluttered carnival where the "ego blooms into an octopus" (Schwartz); the riddle folds back upon the Heraclitean fire, where each one, turning into his own depths, confronts the new either/or: to become flame/or to become cinder.[93]

In much the same way Kierkegaard's "night of the Absolute" remains trapped in the outside (Hegelian) language, and only propels us with Camus upon the absurd "night of Gethsemane"—which is not so absurd after all. It may, if we are open, lead to that "night of universal blossoming" of which Rilke wished to be the minstrel—"a baptist of this new messiahship."

[93] Philip Wheelright, *op. cit.*, pp. 81–82.

Four

ART

Stages in the Act of Becoming

ROGER ORTMAYER

On the opening night of one of the last important exhibitions organized by the lamented Dallas Museum of Contemporary Art, some two hundred patrons, socialites, and educators took hold of a heavy hemp rope at nearly two-foot intervals as marked by gingham bows. Led by an apparition that looked like nothing so much as a living "Mask of Fear" by Paul Klee, they solemnly left the museum building, played follow the leader across the parking lot and down a dark alley, past some back-lot outbuildings where apparitions out of vintage Hallowe'en nights scraped shingles off the roofs, squirted hoses, and emitted a variety of squeaks and squawks. The group finally made its way to a vacant house, where, still clutching the rope, they were led around hallways, up and down stairways, catching glimpses of surrealistic vignettes through opened doors and windows. Some were soon bored: "Let's get out of this and get a drink!" Others persevered in drifting around and around through the house, but looking for something to happen, for after all, they had come to the opening with the expectation of participating in a "happening." Others hoped for some symbolic illumination: "What does it mean?" A few were furious: "And they call this *art*!"

Back at the museum, the entry to the exhibition was through Claes Oldenburg's "Store." Others of the movement in art soon to be tagged as "Pop" were represented; Jimmy Dine and Roy Lichtenshein and the slightly older generation avant-garde such as Jasper Johns and Robert Rauschenberg. The title of the exhibition was "1961." It was a carefully assembled collection of the art produced at the beginning of the sixties. Pop art, not yet so called, was there in splendid force. With typical prescience, director Douglas MacAgy had selections of what would be successively championed as "Op," "Pop," and "Kinetic" art. Also present were somewhat more established, at that moment, masters such as Robert Motherwell with a magnificent "Voyage," an epoxy impregnated "Fat Man" by Robert Mallary, a scintillating post-abstract-expressionism Diebenkorn, a wondrously active but going nowhere Tinguely, an ironic "Apotheosis of St. Joan" by Botero. The show was not large, but in the evidences of artistic freedom and rebellion, in meanings dislocated from classical categories, in art as experience rather than art as illustration, it was an evidence of a certain "triumph" of existentialist expression. Nor was the Dallas exhibition atypical of what was happening on the art scene as the second half of the twentieth century gained momentum.

If generalizations were not so abhorrent to existentialists, one might generalize that most examples of vital painting and sculpture in the second half of the twentieth century are "expressions of existentialism."

I. THE COLLAPSE OF CLASSICAL DISTINCTIONS

The claim that a work of art is an imitation of nature has undergirded most of the classicist assertions of art.

Classicism exploited both aspects of the position: (1) Art, by its very nature, was an imitation, i.e., a representation, an illustration, a copy of something else. Generally nature and man's relation to nature. (2) Nature was best realized through the mechanism of optics and appropriated by the artist-craftsman through the skills of his craft into a naturalistic representation.

Underlying both, however, were assumptions regarding the reality of which nature itself was a copy and an accompanying aesthetic which judged the artist's models by an ideal perfection. Appropriate standards were considered essential for evaluation of works of art: standards of excellence in craftsmanship, realization of hierarchies of value, categories of harmony and balance, naturalistic *verism* matched with idealistic realization.

Because the work of art was representation, its content or subject matter was easily translated into literary terms. The work of art told a story, interpreted an event or a person, or was an allegory useful for purposes of moral edification. The meaning of a work of art was assumed to be identical with its content.

The classicist's assertions made the search for definitions seem to be a valid pursuit and systems of categories inevitable. Art could be domesticated by descriptive explanation; it could be regularized by pigeonholing: sacred vs. secular, subjective vs. objective, profane or religious, of the heart or mind, representing heaven or hell, good or bad, romantic or classical. All "good" art was neat, predictable, and amenable to discursive categories. Evaluation was always loaded on the side of the objective and logical. In the classical systems the irrational was nearly a synonym for the bad; the mind was naturally more to be trusted than the wayward heart, just as the objective was always of higher order than the vagaries of the subjective. That which was amenable to systemization was more to be cherished than the eccentric particular.

Even at its most rational, however, painting and sculpture could never shuck off its existential character. Leonardo's image from a mirror was suffused by the mysterious *sfumato*. The high Renaissance craftsmanship of Michelangelo's "Vatican Pieta" would resolve itself into the existential anguish of the "Rondanini Pieta." Poussin's architectonic layouts would excite the romantic imagination as did the eighteenth-century landscapes of Constable.

What has happened in art in the last three generations, however, has not been simply to exalt the innate existentialism in all art, but effectively to demolish many of the bastions of classicism's structure. It is no longer even possible to define art except in vague generalities. One may speak of art in terms of what it does, provide descriptive materials about the artists and their works, even analyze it in terms of social impact; but to pigeonhole it by a neat definition is no longer attempted except by a few stray academics who may accede to their students' plaintive cries for an outline. Aesthetics is today an area of debate only among the academicians.

The classical principles of separation have been largely obliterated. In their place one encounters situations and constructions characteristic of the existentialist revolt. The faces of Rouault's Christ merge with those of clowns, prostitutes workers, and judges. The separations of secular and sacred vanish altogether in a Lebrun "Dachau Pit," which speaks of the transformation of man in the executioner's chamber. The whole realm of existence becomes the arena in which the action takes place. Christ, e.g., is presented not in definition or out there, not up there, not in a separated realm from this earth. The artist reveals Him as murdered, crucified, abandoned, or reborn. He is not an abstraction, no eternal truth, not a philosophical construction. There is not even argument about his existence. He is simply presented, forsaken, or mourned as dead.

The works of art are encountered as stages in the act of becoming, not finished, final models of a finite reality. They slough off their frames and stretch to sizes so huge there are few buildings to accommodate them. Or they are fragments in process, studies that cannot be finished, provisional glimpses which the artist abandons. They move about in assorted shapes and dimensions, unlike anything ever seen, unrecognizable as shapes the eye has ever gazed upon. They metamorphose, mutate, die and are reborn, rejecting fixed polarities and preconceived images.

The work of art has won its freedom from dependence upon literary forms. It has been able to slough off the traditional accouterments of content. It becomes an entity in itself, not an illustration dependent upon some other story, event or personage. The form of the work of art is its content.

The cherished cliché of classical criticism, that of aesthetic distance, tends to disappear. New works often require a mode of participation impossible when considered by rigidly objective standards. The patron is no longer spectator in the sense of standing apart in objective isolation and analyzing the work by preconceived principles of appreciation. His response is geared to his participation. The work of art becomes a living creation, not only a conceptualized thing. External authority tends to disintegrate. If the artist is queried about the meaning of a certain work, he may turn the question back upon the viewer: "What does it mean to you?" Objectification, however, continues as a desirable factor, but it is called "alienation" instead of aesthetic distance. While it is a device for placing at a distance for evaluation in relation to other aspects of the world, the implication is active and relational rather than passive and isolated.

The preconceived image of the classicist scheme built

from sketches and preliminary drawings to the finished canvas. Oppositely, the existentialist artist has developed a spontaneous, sudden burst of painting activity. Nothing is conceptualized in advance, nothing planned. The act of painting can become the work of art.

Academic training, a necessary accouterment to the older art, has largely disintegrated. In 1959, before Pop art was "in," I met with some of the artists who would soon become its leaders: Jimmy Dine, Alan Kaprow, Claes Oldenburg, Robert Whitman. They were busy putting on "happenings" in lofts in downtown New York City, arranging their environmentals in the Judson and Ruben Galleries, and generally thumbing their noses at the dominant abstract expressionist artists of the New York School. We talked about art in general and their own activities. In the conversation I inquired about their background and training. Dine was from Cincinnati and had received formal training in the art school there as well as in Cleveland. Kaprow was a college teacher, academically trained. Oldenburg was from the Yale School of Art. Then one of them pointed to Whitman: "He's the lucky one. No art school training at all. He doesn't have to unlearn all the junk the rest of us have to!"

II. REBELLION AND FREEDOM

And now what happens with art? Art has been considered since the Greeks to have as its goal the creation of beautiful lines and beautiful color harmonies. If one abolishes this notion, what becomes of art?

I am going to tell you. Art then returns to its real function, much more significant than creating shapes and colors agreeable for a so-called pleasure of the eyes.—JEAN DUBUFFET[1]

The Dadaist . . . acts instinctively, just as a man might say he was a thief out of "Passion," or a stamp-collector by preference. The

[1] Jean Dubuffet, exhibition catalogue, Dallas Museum of Fine Arts, March 16–April 17, 1966, p. 43.

"ideal" has shifted: the abstract artist has become (if you insist, dear reader) a wicked materialist, with the abstruse characteristic of considering the care of his stomach and stock jobbing more honorable than philosophy. "But that's nothing new," those people will shout who can never tear themselves away from the "old." But it is something startlingly new, since for the first time in history the consequence has been drawn from the question: What is German culture? (Answer: Shit), and this culture is attacked with all the instruments of satire, bluff, irony and finally, violence.—RICHARD HUELSENBECK[2]

Already in New York in 1919 I began to react to the Renaissance sense of space and order. I felt keenly that space should be freer. As I remember, I really wanted to smash form, to melt it in a more moving and dynamic way.—MARK TOBEY[3]

About any place one dips into the developments of art in America, he will collide with rebellious artists in struggle against the presanctified forms and constructions of official art. Some have argued that the marvelous French invention was the Academy—it always gave the artist something to fight against. Certainly the dominance of the so-called School of Paris in the first half of this century gives some credence to that claim. The Academy stood there in its immutable and unmovable orthodoxy, always available for attack. Officialdom, institutionalized in the Academy, made the alternatives almost imperative.

This rebellion has been totally radical in an existentialist sense. In the person of one or another of the artists, through their erratic forming, reforming, disintegrating, and reshaping groups and movements, they called into question and directly, often brutally, attacked all the schemes of systemization, representation, and laws of beauty that had been built up through centuries in Western culture. As these ap-

[2] Richard Huelsenbeck: *En Avant Dada: A History of Dadaism (1920)* in Robert Motherwell (ed.), *The Dada Painters and Poets: An Anthology,* (New York: Wittenborn, Schultz, 1951), p. 44.

[3] Mark Tobey, letter to Katherine Kuh, published in Katherine Kuh, *The Artist's Voice* (New York: Harper & Row, 1962), p. 240.

plied to the structures of art, they not only tore down existing orders, they replaced them with novel images in dimensions, shapes, lines and colors and combinations never before imagined.

While the revolts were against various bastions of academicism, they were always for a new and existent freedom of expression.

> Be by turns
> Romantic
> Fauve
> Cubist
> Orphist
> Futurist
> Rhomboidist
> Classical tomorrow—why not?
> See how rich you are
> My dear son!
> I am but a will-o-the-wisp
> Which trembles in the wind and vanishes
> Then is reborn once
> To vanish forever.
> There are also difficult victories
> Very somber defeats
> And famous retreats
> More glorious than victories
> Blessed meditations
> Long infinite patiences
> Dumb victims
> Thanksgiving after childbirth
> And obscure loves
> In this beloved art.
> Some are pampered
> Others excommunicated
> But no matter—provided your heart
> Unhappy artist
> Keeps holiday![4]

[4] From *Soliloques*, Neuchatel, *Ides et Calendes*, 1944. In Courthion, Rouault, New York, Harry N. Abrams, Inc., 1961, p. 400.

For some, Rouault's image of the pilgrimage may be more appropriate than that of rebellion, but it, too, is an existentialist approach, a seeking of that holiday where the artist was the celebrant at an altar quite different from the refuge of the traditional aesthetic sanctuary.

The most spectacular frontal attack upon the fortress of the sanctified, which resulted in a liberating freedom for exploration by the artist, was mounted by the Dadaists. They were superb iconoclasts, delightedly smashing every cherished art form, thumbing their nose at all conventions, fervent in anger and fulminations against the enemy (everything revered as "art" or "culture"), and yet, in the strange economy of the creative they not only succeeded in liberating the artist to a new freedom, but created new images and forms which often are commonplace today. The Dadaist explosion exposed the meretricious and phony values of conventional classicism. They stood bourgeois art on its head by painting moustaches on reproductions of "Mona Lisa," exhibitionist tricks such as Duchamp's, placing a urinal in an art exhibition and titling it "Eternal Spring." While they displayed the vulgar and called it art, suddenly it became apparent that much of what had been classified as beautiful was simply empty pretentiousness, a fatuous pattern of bourgeois snobbery, and in nonart objects (bicycle wheels, bottle holders, combs, table utensils) there emerged exciting energies and marvelous contours.

As with many of the art movements, the Dadaists were more centrifugal in their energies than cohesive as a group. The movement started with a few disgusted refugees from wartime conscription in the First World War, ashamed of any identification with the outrages of war. Mostly from France and Germany, and as with Arp, from the between-land of Alsace, they found each other in neutral Switzerland. Pacifists as far as the war was concerned, they were bitterly hostile to all sequences of political, economic, and social order under whose pretentious and spurious banners the slaughter was justified. They delighted in the individual as against societal, political, or military castes. In confusion they found value. Anarchy was a positive force against the hierarchies of power. They sought to inhabit in reality, not simply illusion, the landscape of the absurd. They postulated the sequences of the absurd as against the logic of cause and effect.

While the mood was anarchic, the effect was satirical and ironic. While the attack seemed nihilist in its destructive temper, the images they produced by means of random association and deliberate dissociation created free forms, collages, and assemblages which not only made meaningless the classical distinctions of two-dimensional and three-dimensional art but also created notable new works out of incongruous materials and images which have freed art for exciting new structures and compositions in diverse fields. They delighted in the experience of destruction and creation.

The Dadaists enhanced human existence. Their thoroughgoing rebellion gave a freedom to the artist as creator-spectator and to the patron a role as spectator-participant which could never have been achieved in the old order.

Surprisingly, Dadaist exhibitionism resulted in a new way of seeing the art work. From their disorder came a refreshing level of order which, as we shall note, involved a pattern of relationship to nature with fascinating parallels to what the avant-garde among the speculative scientists were also exploring. Their immersion in the particularities of concrete existence shook out much of the preciousness and metaphysical mumbo-jumbo from the self-conscious fine arts. In fact, after Dada, the use of such a term as "fine art" became so embarrassingly pedantic that it has almost disappeared. Their venturesome explorations into the art use of spontaneity, while certainly not originated by the Dadaists, produced such vigorous and unexpected twists that nearly a half century later new experiments are extolled only to discover that the Dadaists had dipped into nearly the same area during their brief moment. They brought back into art a releasing sense of play in art. Their insults often bordered on a kind of joyous celebration. Their contempt of the official was a bill of rights to the individual rebel to assert himself. Their attempts at confusion through juxtaposing seemingly unrelated arts in simultaneous concert helped to batter down the rigid compartments of tradition and through free association gave to poetry and cinema, drama and painting, sculpture and music an interplay of which even now we have been able to realize only the most faint possibilities.

III. TREMENDOUS FRAGMENTS OF MEANING

In his 1924 lecture to the Jena Kunstverein, Paul Klee discussed, in appropriately oblique fashion, something of the way in which life is given to a painting through the interrelationship of the formal means of "measure," "weight," and "quality." It was when he related these standard concepts to color, tone, and line that it was seen that the old formalities really were not being applied at all; or in a more accurate sense, they were being applied radically as ends in themselves. The meaning had shifted.

He went on to discuss color as a mode of expression, color as tonal and color as constructive, and then he suddenly inserted a typically Klee observation: "Tremendous fragments of meaning."[5]

The "fragments of meaning," as a Klee painting or drawing always shows, are in the color, line, and tone, not in external truths, stories, illustrations, or anecdotes. And the meanings are not generalizations but, rather, glimpses, glimmers, fractions, and excerpts or, to quote Klee again, "Merrily dancing tears."

5 Paul Klee, "On Modern Art," 1924, lecture in Jena, published in 1945.

They are unique meanings, for they inhere in the work, not in what the work is all about. Even though his pastorales and cityscapes may have been attempts to take nature apart and rebuild it into new models of the world and nature, they were done not to point out truths about the nature of nature but as experiences in which the meaning adhered in the work itself and the experience of the work instead of ideograms of what nature might be like. Klee insisted that he revised nature in order that nature might be reborn.

Klee furthered what Cézanne began. Cézanne's passionate attention to volume and mass was an exploration of nature as transformed into the autonomous world of art. His painting was not about its subject matter. Instead he sought to realize (*réaliser*) nature in the work of art by closing the gap between nature and form. He did this by taking form seriously and making himself, as artist and human being, to be identified with the pictorial work. Thereby, as the sense of form was intensified, human existence was realized in relation to the work of art.

Cézanne and Klee both used formal means toward a kind of realization contrary to the traditional uses of such techniques. Classicism utilized the formal techniques of the painter as means toward another end, i.e., the preconceived subject matter of the work. Volumes and planes were gimmicks for establishing the hierarchies of value by which the story would be told. Cézanne did not use spheres and cones as tricks to say something else; he freed them as pictorial ends in themselves. Klee moved the process toward its radical conclusion. He gave them movement and the viewer could realize them as works in process, yet the paintings were complete in being their own content. His paintings exist as fragments of meaning, but not in the sense that they are building blocks for some overarching whole. While each work may be partial and fragmentary, it is a dip into the teeming variety of existence and each glimpse is worth whatever any other glimpse is worth. Existential value does not assign degrees of worth to life. Life, whenever authentic, is its own justification. No work of art, just as no construct of man, can ever be total in meaning. Existentialism does not seek the comfort of absolutes. All meanings are partial, as in a Klee painting.

It is at the point of "meaning" that many have difficulty with existentialist art. So infused is Western culture with quantitative language structures, cause and effect sequences, rational development in logical argument that when a citizen is confronted by language continuities which are presented in simultaneity rather than a chain of sequences, with fragmentary glimpses rather than causal continuities, with emotive actions rather than rational development, he tends to find the situation meaningless. He has been trained to believe that only rational sequences carry meaning and that arational or irrational structures are synonyms for meaninglessness.

In the old system of categories, that art which opposed the static rationality of classicism was labeled "romantic." The romantic cherished the emotive, romantic artists bathed in feeling and washed up works of Dionysiac energy and unbridled passion. Today many academicians disparage the existentialist revolt as simply another surge of romanticism from which we will one day recover and with equilibrium resume the placid course of classicism. Huntington Hartford even built a New York museum to back up such a belief.

This contention might be taken more seriously if the present developments were but the reverse side of the coin of classicism. Romanticism, historically, has been a part of an accepted whole. Romantics believed in the same world as the classicists, they put the emphasis differently. Dionysus and Apollo both were at home on Olympus; they had inhabited the same pantheon. While it is true that the new arts exhibit many of the patterns of romanticism, the surface coincidences should not deceive us.

What has happened today is more like the war of the

Titans, in which an entirely new order has challenged an existing authority. There is simply no way for man to move back to the eighteenth century, the fifteenth or the fifth century B.C. Man's relation to nature has undergone such a radical reshaping that it is nonsense to dream about returning to the olden times—except in nostalgia, and if there is anything that should be avoided by the existentialist it is the cliché, the first-born of nostalgia.

Existentialism has attempted to authenticate human existence at a time when the psyche has often lost its bearings. Existentialism has moved in at those points where anxiety and dread have been inflamed by the threat of nonbeing and the deflation or failure of external supports, i.e., the death of God. All the "laws" of the fixed universe have fallen. The new mode is not simply a counterpoint to the classical rules; it is a new universe in which process has superseded finality and the person is always turned back upon himself as the cutting edge of discovery.

Just as, theologically, existentialism has helped modern man to free faith from dependence upon accouterments, so the artist has presented him with works which are parallels to that required of man—i.e., glimpses of self-authenticating existence. In art the form is the content (no external verities required), and in the person it is personal decision with absolutely nothing external to sustain. There is no way out for the human being except his humanity, and that is not a way out but a recognition of what it is to be alive. The art has no "standards" by which it can be evaluated, other than those which inhere in the work itself.

This inner dependence of the work of art is like freedom, however; it is easily misinterpreted. As Sartre insisted, "Man *is* his freedom." Even so, a painting or a sculpture is its content. Man in his freedom is always in relation and a work of art is always in situation. It has analogies, associations; it may relate to myth, even be a symbol. But one must watch sign-making activity, it easily degenerates into allegory. Allegory is usually an existentialist betrayal, a way of allowing pseudo-rational accouterments to take over and define the work.

IV. THE EXPERIENCE OF ART

Art as personal experience is as religion in terms of worship rather than theology. In this sense, in whatever mode or tradition, art has demanded an existential relationship. It is irrefutably personal. No one can experience the "Mona Lisa" or Franz Kline's "Wanamaker Block" for another person. A critic's discussion or even the camera's reproduction is no substitute for the personal experience. Only *you* (or *I*) can worship; only *you* (or *I*) can experience a work of art. No one can do it for us.

Just as the "form of art is its content" has forced us to deal with the art work itself rather than the art as illustration of some truth or absolute external to itself, so we have been forced to experience art in itself, not art as moral uplift, patriotic illustration, propagandistic effort, or literary allegory. That which has always been true of valid art now becomes an obligation. The work of art demands recognition as experience, not allegory.

Franz Kline's "Wanamaker Block" is not *about* the Wanamaker building or square any more than his "Bethlehem" is about the steel-making city in Pennsylvania or his "Dahlia" is a reproduction of a certain type of domesticated flower. "Wanamaker Block" is a painting, not an illustration. The artist, as was usually the case with his paintings, gave his canvas the title "Wanamaker Block" sometime after he had finished working on it. The title may not have been solely capricious, but it had nothing to do with a naturalistic or even an expressionistic reproduction, or allegories about the New York City square. The same relation applied to all the later Kline paintings.

. . . these are painting experiences. I don't decide in advance that I'm going to paint a definite experience, but in the act of painting, it becomes a genuine experience for me. It's not symbolism any more than it's calligraphy. I'm not painting bridge constructions, skyscrapers or laundry tickets. . . . I don't paint objectively. . . . I don't paint a given object—a figure or a table; I paint an organization that becomes a painting.[6]

The actionist New York School of painters, to which Kline "belonged" and which was dominant in the fifteen years following the Second World War, faced many curious and ill-informed accusations such as "impersonal," "abstract," "esoteric," "antihuman." Such criticism must have come from the observers' failure to find in the paintings those "values" they had been convinced belonged to the humanist tradition; the images did not have the contours of familiar and visible objects and therefore they must be abstractions. Because the canvases were strange and odd in style they could be termed "esoteric," which usually carried with it overtones of perversion. In the paintings there were no recognizable lines or volumes that spelled out the objective appearance of the human figure in the tradition of Titian or Boucher. Since the figure in its objective outlines was not impressed upon the retina of the eye, *ergo*, it was not present.

A more penetrating observation of the works would have come up with opposite descriptive observations. A painting such as "Wanamaker Block" is frighteningly personal. The artist had to produce it from his very guts; he was given no props such as the rules or laws of painterly construction. He faced a huge, bare canvas and from that nothingness he had to create something. He had nothing to lean on but his own solitary act. The evidence, from the confidences of those artists who have attempted it, is that this moment is of such traumatic intensity that the artist is shaken to the core of existence. Compared to it the building up of an objectively

6 Kuh, *op. cit.*, p. 144.

organized human figure on canvas is as memorizing a poem is to the agony of creating its metaphors. Only much more disturbing, for the actionist painter created *ex nihilo,* from nothing. Theology has traditionally reserved such activity only for God, and threatened with destruction those who attempted God's role. There was something almost suicidal in the work of Kline, Pollock and Gorky. Gorky did commit suicide, and the death of Pollock in an automobile accident was like suicide—racing about the countryside in a high-speed vehicle as if wishing for the death that came. Perhaps it is not possible to create *ex nihilo* without going mad; however, the real madness is in the blindness that could call it "impersonal"!

"Abstract" is another wildly inappropriate designation for such art as that of Kline, *et al.* "Abstraction" is a useful term in describing constructivist work like that of the later Mondrian or the clarity of Britain's Ben Nicholson, possibly sculptors such as Pevsner or a significant portion of Barbara Hepworth's production. "Abstract" carries the connotation of mathematical precision and clarity, of an *abstraction* from life.

There is no abstraction in "Wanamaker Block." It has a fever and brutality quite opposed to the clarity and delicate precision of an abstraction. It is not divorced from life but spells it out in huge capital letters, almost as if Sartre had described it as putting a fist in "the belly where life is." "Abstract expressionism" is not an appropriate term to apply to such art; critic Clement Greenberg was inspired in giving the description of "action painting" to the genre.

Kline insisted that the artist "paints blind," even though, as he often did, he might make quite a number of preliminary sketches. When he did make sketches it was not, however, to predetermine what the final painting might be, but to give him freedom. The sketches were not designs which he enlarged in the final painting, but preliminary fragments which could be combined, and altered, in the final work. They were never determinative. Although Kline worked fast, he insisted that "what goes into a painting isn't just done while you're painting."

Randomness as an integral aspect of painting was christened by Kline as by the whole New York school. When sketches were used in developing a painting they did not lessen the immediacy and impulse of the act of creating, but acted as a further enhancing dynamic.

The style knocked the ends out of aesthetic space. Jackson Pollock's paintings, for instance, have resisted confinement. The process of painting was one of energetic and endless movement. The movement was obsessive, something parallel to a baroque high altar. The parallel can be drawn even further. The painting was as if an altar to the painter.

Pollock's "Cathedral" was given a title which suggests something of the sanctuary, the consecrated shelter or holy place. But he certainly was not painting an object named "cathedral." The internal dynamic of the painting is that of artist Pollock, not the contours of Chartres or St. John the Divine. While it is spontaneous, an invention of the artist, it is also something of an altar. It is Pollock's moment of belief, his testament.

The exoneration of the artist, Pollock, was his deed of art. His own self was his act of painting. He was existentially responsible in his freedom to paint. He did not turn his art into a law for painting, but judged and acted as artist.

A word especially dear to the French religious existentialists might be used—"presence." The painting becomes a presence.

The terms "commitment" and "encounter" are required in discussing action art. The artist becomes a totally responsible person—as artist. It would have been somewhat futile, certainly awkward, to have inquired of either Kline or Pollock just what his responsibility, e.g. to society, might have been. Futile because he could give no answer other than his painting; awkward because it would assume a kind of science of responsibility in the moral sense, when his was an obsession with responsibility as painter. His action was significant as painter, not as moralist. Also his sense of responsibility was as ultimate as a person could make it. He was committed to creating in vital action. His experience was not recollection, nostalgia, recognition of something objective, but a taking on of total responsibility for his action. He could not locate blame or regard in any other person or thing. His act was totally his own responsibility. It was critically his significant and vital action. "Action rather than knowledge," as Kierkegaard put it. He was not painting someone else or about someone else. Or, as de Kooning has said, "an artist could practice his intuitions." The experience was the painting, and also for the patron the experience is the encounter of the painting.

It is always a silly comment to say of an action painting, "It looks like. . . ." It does not look like anything except by coincidence. In itself it can only look like a painting and needs no interpretation than the act of painting for the artist and the encounter with the painting for the viewer. The painter's responsibility has been met in his willingness to be committed to painting. The viewer's responsibility is to be able to participate in the encounter and not twist away with some literary parallel, philosophical discussion, theological excursion, or even aesthetic commentary. The present is all that is needed.

Which may be a weakness of the radical existentialist mode—objective criticism is nearly impossible.

So-called "Op art" is equally an art of experience as is action art, but one which makes more concessions to the plea for an objective sense of order and precision.

More plastic than action art, Op art plays the game with "cool." For what seems like generations Josef Albers, retaining the "elementarism" of his Bauhaus courses, has painted squares upon squares of color. This was about as far from the feverish commitment of expressionism as one might theoretically go. In fact, Albers, in his teaching both at the Bauhaus and at Yale, rigorously demanded the exclusion of all expressionist aims. In its place he wanted rational forms.

But no less than the expressionists, the result was an art of experience. There has been no *Sturm und Drang*, no symbolic struggle with archetypal symbolism, no violent and intuitive action, but the art itself remains the experience, as thoroughly as with the New York School. While an art of abstraction, rather than expression, it is nonetheless an art of experience and renewal. It will allow no convenient literary or illustrative allegories; it is similarly an art of change, recognizing that it is man and man's humaneness that needs transformation. Insists Victor Vasarely:

> The first tantalizing question that people asked me when they saw my abstractions: "But what does it mean . . ." left me perplexed for some time. The question is still asked, but in the course of the years I have found, not *the* answer, but the answers. Objectively speaking, what I paint is a two-dimensional composition of forms-color or a multi-dimensional structure, in which intuition, science and technique all have a share, containing visual stimuli and intended for one of the multiple plastic functions of the modern city. Subjectively speaking, it is a poetic creation having sense qualities, capable of stimulating the imaginative and emotional process in others. On this ground, to be sure, all interpretations or equivalences become possible. There will accordingly spread round my work—which was conceived to be rigorously dialectical—a metaphysical halo imagined, desired, willed by the viewers. I can do nothing about this! For, as far as I am concerned, there was never consciously a theme having as its origin an extra-plastic story or anecdote which I wished to communicate by means of the canvas. Having convinced myself of the vanity of tirelessly representing—as it is done—the named or unnamed archetypes of nature, I wished to create the beings of a world apart, that of pure plastics: genesis, birth, abundance, complexification, perfecting, functionalization of plastic structures.[7]

[7] *Vasarely* (Neuchatel: Editions du Griffon, 1965), p. 74.

Vasarely is the other side of the coin from the actionist painters. Like Albers, he eschews all expressionism, seeking the "objective," as he puts it. He, therefore, is suspicious of subjectivity. But he feels that the work of art must eclipse the artist, that he can create a plastic language in which all extra-plastic elements are superfluous. It is an art for which there is no interpretation; it is an experience in, of, and for itself. Certainly Vasarely's precisionist craftsmanship is in contrast to the impulsive brush of Franz Kline. His hard edge and carefully plotted optical tricks are poles away from Kline's blurred rectangles, blocks, and brutal strokes in which the impressions left by the brush as dragged across the canvas are their own poignant testimony.

Nevertheless, the two artists each have their say in the existentialist rebellion. Kline's work has obvious parallels and the viewer is tempted to give interpretations that correspond to the existentialist themes of dread, anxiety, loneliness, and the absurd. The violence exhibited in the brutal brush work and uncompromising black-and-white color contrasts seemed almost an existentialist lesson. His uncompromising act of creation from nothing was a defiant, if precarious, affirmation of identity, of the artist's selfhood defying the forces of annihilation. Kline's work is received as a cry is heard and evokes violent response and reaction. One, like Camus's "Judge-Penitent," may have heard the cry but hurried on, never to erase from his memory that moment of anguish. Another may have responded with his own act of identity, awakened to his own being, participated in a revelatory moment.

In contrast, Vasarely suggests little of the thematic existentialist approach. In fact he repudiates such expressionist meddling. His art, however, is no less an art of experience than that of Kline. The response is primarily one of sensation. One participates in a Vasarely work, and is similarly forced to be aware of his own identity through the puzzles of appearances and the sensations of movement. The evocative pressure is more intellectual than visceral, but pressure it is, not illustration or object lessons.

In the Chicago Art Institute there hangs a Clifford Still on which "black on black" is dominant. It is a large painting. The contours of the imagery are typically Still—attenuated peaks and valleys. The looming intensity of the black is broken only on one side, by one uncertain line of color. The effect is revelatory, in contrast to the way of seeing in a Vasarely or the direct violence of the creative act of Kline. There is something archetypal in its sensation. In some ways, it is more compelling than the Kline. Kline's work was direct action; the movement was in sensing the act of creation. Still's painting inclines toward action, a movement responded to by the viewer more toward direction than identity. That is, while Kline's violence requires something of a response of being to the artist's own testament of selfhood, the Still moves more as a ritual action, movement with a sense of direction. This symbolic movement is neither so conscious, nor rational as Vasarely, nor so inchoate and violent as Kline. It is both conscious and unconscious, both a giving of clues to rational directions and moving along levels something like those of dreams. Its meaning depends upon the viewer's participation but also exists in its own archetypal imagery. It is symbolic in that it calls the self into awareness, but also it transcends the immediate sensation. Both the world "out there" and the inscape of the self are touched.

V. FROM THE EXPRESSIONIST MODE TO TOTAL EXPERIENCE

Existentialism is resistance to themes as much as it is opposition to abstracted truth. There is no logical reconciliation of the contradictions of art in existentialism. There is no system of existentialist art. It attempts events and acts of truthfulness rather than categories of truth. Nevertheless, certain motifs, even themes are located in existentialist art, just as being truthful is its inspiration.

In the art revolution of the twentieth century, it has been the expressionist wing which has pushed most radically, first, into the new style of art and then, second, into new forms.

The impressionists in their experiments with color as a light-reflecting agent were followed up by the cubists with a similarly objective analysis of perspective, planes, and masses. Their experiments forced a new aesthetic, a reshaped experience of the art object. Their work remained, however, essentially in the classical tradition. They manipulated the laws of art. Their objective was the production of an art object. New ways of seeing were probed into, and the experience of the art work gained vigor which had been largely dissipated by the old academicism. The emphasis remained, however, upon art as an objective pursuit which experimented with new laws and patterns. The end result was an object with, perhaps, a new measure of aesthetic distance from artist and spectator; nevertheless it was a "distance" and the work of art was an "object."

The expressionists, learning much stylistically from the impressionists, and their cubist successors, began to break down the place of the object and replace it with direct experience. Art, in their hands, began to shift from object to relationship. It is this direction which has produced the most essentially existentialist art and the rather heady realization that something unique has been born in our time.

The customary criticism of expressionist art has been a detailing of motifs. Themes such as alienation and disaffiliation, misery and compassion, protest and rebellion, anxiety and loneliness were drawn as analogies seeking to interpret the production of the expressionist artists.

Such an interpretation was sustained by both the works of art and intrinsic facts of the artists' lives. A radical humanism invested most of their work. They involved themselves in social protest in its political and economic aspects as well as in image-making. Expressionist artists were often found working politically with movements of rebellion and change. Hitler, in his attempts to destroy German expressionist art, was motivated not only by his bourgeois standards of what constituted good art, but by a political awareness that the artists who produced it were uncompromising enemies of Nazism. If a senile Nolde be allowed as the exception to the rule, the expressionist artists constituted a rebellious core of opposition to Hitlerism. Their radical humanism was affronted by the human destruction of the Nazis and, when dispersed into the rest of the world by active persecution, served not only to incite opposition to the Nazi wave, but initiated existentialist developments among the intellectuals and artists in their new homes.

Expressionistic developments had been accompanied by turbulent exhibitions and restless and stormy associations. In good existentialist fashion, the developments were dynamic, spurred on by the need to communicate and penetrate into uncharted areas of the human condition. Fragmentation accompanied excited controversy but stimulated new groupings of which Brücke and Blaue Reiter came to significant fruition. All were infused by a joy in personal expression, even if the themes were of misery and desperation.

Expressionistic art was aggressive. In 1907 Emil Nolde wrote a friend: ". . . If I may offer you a piece of good advice . . . it would be this: If you discern a lawlessness, free will, excessive license, roughness, or brutality in these contemporary works, then study them long and carefully, and you will, in the end, realize how this apparent license becomes liberty, and roughness becomes refinement. Inoffensive pictures of any value are rare."[8]

[8] Quoted by Umbro Apollonio in *Encyclopedia of World Art*, V (New York: McGraw-Hill Book Company, 1961), p. 315.

From the violence of Munch's "The Cry" to the disturbing symbolism of Beckmann's "The Departure," expressionist art wedded visions of reality of the world outside to a poetic inward view of the self. Wilhelm Wöller, a participant in the historic exhibition smashed by Hitler's storm troopers, found refuge first in Brazil and later in New York City. His Brazilian watercolors are full of jungle creatures and exotic flora, but mostly they are Wöller's self-vision. After coming to New York, he worked in the early days of television, before his death, as a scene painter. A recently exhibited group of his offhours paintings shows that at some points he became nostalgic, e.g., painting recollections of Tyrol with sharp peaks and baroque churches, but while the images are Tyrolean in content, the contours are nostalgia. To view them is not to be given a nostalgic illustration but an experience of nostalgia itself. Nevertheless, the agent for the sentiment is an art object. To move on and be able to discard reliance upon the art object and yet maintain the experienced relationship of art has been one of the real extensions of contemporary existentialism in art. And an acerbating source of irritation to the traditionalists.

Predictably, the Dadaists explored some of the terrain. Their anarchic sessions and exhibitions evoked predictable howls of anger and derision. The confusion fired by insulting manifestoes and recriminations heated up the atmosphere of their portion of the art world. The experience of confrontation was often much more exciting than the works of art themselves. In fact, it was the transmutation of the art object that was the source of much of the experience. The art object as a self-conscious representation of nature, determined by rationalized rules and preconceptions, filled with a content of meaning of proper literary proportions was derided and ridiculed. In its place Duchamp placed objects themselves, ready-mades such as a miniature urinal in the 1917 Independents' exhibition titled "Fountain" by "R. Mutt," hatracks and garden tools, as well as constructions put together from the world of commonplace experience.

Succeeded by the surrealists, Dada destroyed itself. Its self-destruction was as if programed and a prototype of the experience of art violence endemic in the existentialist revolt.

The experience of violence and autodestruction is usually interpreted by those repulsed by its irrationality and threatened by the disintegration of forms in place of a supposed permanence and stability, as a symbol, or model, of the world. Accustomed to think of art as an imitation of nature, they see the experience of violence as an interpretation of what the artist considers the world itself to be like. There is, of course, a sense in which this supposition has some support, but more importantly, such preconceptions are booby traps. They will not let art be art, but always want to transpose it into some rational proposition or concept, even if the concept be that of destruction. They comprehend a philosophy of destruction. For example, they feel they can cope with a philosophy of nihilism. They have conceptualized nothingness, which is quite a trick in itself. A philosophy of irrationality is forced into the categories of rational order.

The art of violence and destruction has helped us to get away from art as philosophy or a model of the universe. It is an experienced relationship. It is an event. Rather than a thing seen and evaluated, it is an occurrence experienced.

It does seem as if, in these days of television, the newscasters can count on artists to help them out when they are looking for a laugh. As I write this, I have just been watching a newscast taped in London. The place was Covent Garden. The camera zoomed in on a man playing a piano. After a few tinny notes, he was joined by a companion who came on camera carrying an ax or a sledge hammer, I could not make out the exact implement. The player jumped from his seat and, grabbing a similar weapon, joined the newcomer in an attack on the piano and bench. In a few moments they had reduced it to a pile of shattered junk; the newscaster made an ironic comment about the state of art, and the program cut to Vietnam.

The juxtaposition of art violence and official destructiveness was obvious, although nobody was making jokes about Vietnam. The demolition of a musical instrument and the demolishing of a village have certain ritual parallel. One, however, was art and the other was . . . politics? morals? statesmanship?

The art of violence possesses a kind of responsibility humanity wishes the statesmen possessed. The artist is reasonably clear on this: ". . . destruction has no place in society—it belongs to our dreams; it belongs to art."[9]

When art had a single focus, viz., the art object, the experience tended to become static; a condition parallel to the frozen movement, the stasis, of the art object. The discovery of art as a relationship, an experience, underlies much of the autodestruction and violence encountered in happenings.

The existentialists have insisted that it is relationships, not things, that count for human beings. Reality is not a proposition to be understood, but "an extended network of relationships, a juxtaposition of events. It was something that needed to be experienced."[10]

The artist needed a different language from his inheritance of easel painting and sculptured three-dimensional objects. The twentieth century's unique contribution to art, the motion picture, was one development. The picture was unfrozen. Its humble origins in the nickelodeon and two-reelers shown in unprententious, workingman's quarters fortunately kept it alive as experience and out of the hands of the self-conscious art dilettantes who would probably have frozen the new forms to death. Fortunately they were

9 Ralph Ortiz in *Art and Artists*, Vol. 1, No. 5 (August, 1966), p. 60.

10 Kenneth Coutts-Smith, in "Violence in Art," *Art and Artists*, Vol. 1, No. 5 (August, 1966), p. 5.

absorbed with their struggles against innovations in the traditional genre and could pretend that the cinema was not art, therefore unworthy of notice.

Throughout the whole development of contemporary art, as familiar traditions disintegrate under cubist and expressionist rebellions, there seems to have been an awareness that something more than the reshaping of the art object was required. It continued to push outside its frames, obliterating the distinctions between two-dimensional and three-dimensional arts in a melding that was neither painting nor sculpture and something other than the sum of both inheritances. The futurists tried to destroy the "cult of the past" with a glorification of movement and technology; the surrealists probed into "surreality" by probing into subconscious, spontaneous, and irrational configurations; the supremists sought to free art and artists from all "sociological or material associations"; the neoprimitivists tried to recapture something of the naïveté of a child's delight in things; the action painters moved toward the experience of creating as being the work of art.

All these developments required participation, from both artist and spectator. As spectators kept being drawn into the act, it happened that the gallery took on something of a theatrical aspect, an occasion for *events* rather than a showcase for things. The "happening" was born.

Early in the spring of 1960, the garden of the Museum of Modern Art in New York was the stage for one of Tinguely's spectacles. He had put together a white-painted assemblage about twenty-three feet long and twenty-seven feet high made up of the odd combinations found by a diligent combing of junkyards in the vicinity of Manhattan: a baby bath and a piano, claxons and electric motors, etc. Then early one evening a prestigous company of museum officials, art patrons and artists gathered and in twenty-eight minutes the assemblage succeeded in destroying itself with a variety of noisy, smelly and vigorous actions, assisted by firemen called in when a fire extinguisher in the piano threatened to explode.

On the one hand, the event could be labeled a parable of our world, with many apt if odious parallels. On the other, it could be a kind of self-conscious exhibitionism. The artist himself thought it "beautiful beyond description."

As in the happening at the Dallas Museum, the old aesthetic categories are irrelevant for criticism or analysis. The object is only a part of the event, the relationship experience is the focus. As Kenneth Coutts-Smith says, "Aesthetic experience is now a matter of participation, a three-way dialogic situation actually taking place in space and time between the artist, the spectator, and the object. It is something that *happens,* in which one is actively and psychologically involved rather than something you look at and take on subjectively."[11]

The art object will not go away. Autodestructive art is only a phase, passing, perhaps. Red Groom's painting of the fire remains from one of the first "happenings," organized and created after he had encountered a Manhattan fire with all the color, noise, and dread of the event. Jackson Pollock's canvases are a continuing treasure years after his death. The dialogue continues to turn three corners of creator, object, and spectator—but the emphasis has switched from the professional craftsmanship of the object to the relationship of the art object and its creative birth with spectator-participant and artist-participant.

VI. SO WHAT?

The accelerating fusion and disintegration of art categories, which the existentialist rebellion has stimulated, has brought art to a precarious balance which the existentialist

11 *Ibid.*

may say is good but which results in much anxiety and irritation for most people. The venerable European tradition, initiated by the Greeks and revived by the Renaissance thinkers and artists, that the work of art ought properly to be a unique synthesis of intense intellectual activity and skilled craftsmanship, does not die easily. The results of that wedding, i.e., splendid works of art which by their presence are inspirations to the human spirit, are looked upon as evidences of the supreme achievements of the human spirit. When brought together in collections such as the Prado, the Louvre, the Uffizi, and the Metropolitan, they serve not just as depositories of the history of taste and craftsmanship, but as shrines.

Putting a moustache on "Mona Lisa" becomes an act of impiety. It is an attack upon the fundamental structures of self-realization. The predictable results are recrimination and outrage. And so the lines are drawn between those who insist that art must eventuate in the art object as the realization of the best activity of mind and craft in a hierarchy of aesthetic values, and those for whom the emphasis is upon art experience as fundamental to existential awareness.

It would be easy, however, if the lines were so simply drawn. Art, in the Western world, has always been cherished because of its revelatory power. At this point, the existentialist emphasis upon art as expressive of human need and hope is not alien to the classical. The division comes with the existentialist claim that the artist must deal with what is life rather than rationalistic abstractions from life. There is a difference between Goya's "The Disasters of War" and the way in which a French classicist painter of the same period would deal with similar material. Picasso, whatever period, usually speaks to the human condition, and some claim this puts him in the Renaissance tradition in spite of his primitivism. Klee and Kandinsky, who initiated the decisive break with classical continuities, matured just about the time that perceptive museum men were collecting Van Gogh and Gauguin for their shrines. The Bauhaus partners moved the painting away from being about anything. It was no pictorial representation of nature, even when labeled a landscape. Its message was itself, not *about* something else. It took the emphasis away from inward brooding, the motivation for expressionism, and forced consideration of the work of art itself, allowing few, if any, literary, sociological, or psychological interpretations. This would seem to have been a step toward classicism, but it was not. Classicism rested much of its case upon art as a particular realization of universal truths, something quite horrifying to existentialist claims. Klee's drawings were autonomous realizations, as were Kandinsky's improvisations. They would start with a dot and a line; the end was unpredictable from the original stroke. If there was a generalization to be made, it was in the *process,* not the abstracted aphorism.

Others attacked the very conception of fine art, the identification of the art object as having some special kind of nonutilitarian existence. They moved objects, anything associated with the human experience, into a kind of consideration in which relatedness, or nonrelatedness, was emphasized rather than an analysis or criticism of the object. In fact, the object might be destroyed so that the experience of relationship might be enhanced. Curiously, this emphasis came along with the utter dissociation of self and object.

It is futile to attempt a prediction of coming trends. One can suggest, however, that art in the predictable future will not go back to the classicism dominant since the Renaissance. The existentialist thrust has been too deep, its revolt too violent ever to go back. The formulas consecrated by classicism have lost out, even as clichés.

Intellectualism is not dead, even in autodestructive art. Among many who delight in the art object as such, it is reasserting itself against expressionist brooding and murky structures.

In spite of the disintegration of distinctive forms of art in general, specialties persist. Easel painting, for example, is reasserting itself. The same is true of sculpture and the graphics.

But new routes keep moving in at an amazing rate. Happenings and environmentals are not going out of style —even though in 1961 some of their imitators spoke of them as passé. The musicians and the poets keep joining up with the painters and the sculptors, and they all go on stage, where the dramatist thought he had territory staked out, or they create films which themselves are works of art rather than attempts to be about art.

Perhaps it is even fruitless to attempt a coherent criticism of existentialist effects in art. Such an effort would presuppose a theoretical basis which the existentialist would immediately deride as being irrelevant. Nevertheless, theoretical bases for analysis are not that easily disposed of, and it may well be that uneasiness in the midst of seeming existentialist anarchy will demand and reassert a rationally coherent structure in evaluating art forms. Unquestionably, the human being to whom art activity seems an integral part of his existence will continue to resist the totally subjective, anarchistic, transient, and fragmented art developments. He develops a counterpassion for objectivity, rational order, permanence, and coherence to be symbolized in works of art. Art will continue to assert a speculative and rational character, there can be no question about that.

Nevertheless, it has been the essentially existentialist spirit which has given to modern art the drive to break with the past. The result is one of the most exciting and pervasive developments in the entire history of man. The first half of the twentieth century, by any possible assessment, has been the stage for one of the most staggering arts developments ever seen on this planet. In terms of size, momentum, initiation of the unique, influence in all realms of existence, and startling creative output, no other period in history comes close. It has also forced a reassessment of the word "art." It cannot revert to its former restrictive usage. For the foreseeable future we will not attempt definitions of art. We will be forced to deal with it in terms of what it does.

Five

PSYCHOLOGY

Existentialism, Psychotherapy, and the Problem of Death

ROLLO MAY

On March 1, 1966, Mayor John V. Lindsay appointed New York City's first Narcotics Coordinator. There were two things that made this event more interesting than the usual routine appointment. One was that the young psychiatrist appointed, Dr. Efren Ramirez, had already been known in the profession by rumor across the water from Puerto Rico, where he was director of the Addictions Research Center. He had been able to achieve, so the rumor had it, what almost no one else in the profession has been able to accomplish, namely psychotherapy with that most difficult of all patients, the narcotics addict, with some hope of effective "cure."

The second aspect of special interest was that Dr. Ramirez accomplished this on the basis of existential principles. The *New York Times* article noted that he "blended existentialism into his psychiatry." After he had been, in college, "fascinated by the existentialist views of Sartre and Camus and the possibilities of their application to psychiatry," he had gone on to medical training and internship at the Columbia Presbyterian Medical Center. Then after serving as medical officer in the United States Air Force, he had begun to "hone his existentialist approach to psychiatry," particularly in the treatment of addiction.

"I will tell an addict," the *Times* reporter quoted Dr. Ramirez' description of his approach, "I am a doctor. I'm not responsible for your being an addict. I can merely offer you the alternatives to take you out of the hole. The rest is up to you."

Dr. Ramirez' appointment, and his work, are one evidence of the effective seeping into American psychology and psychiatry of existentialist influence. This evidence—and a number of other incidents of this existential influence could be cited—is particularly relevant since it follows the initial period of a paradoxical attitude in American psychology and psychiatry to the existential approach.

Let us begin by exploring that paradox. On one hand, there had been a good deal of overt interest in this area among psychiatrists and psychologists. Meetings on the topic at professional conventions overflowed. There was also genuine conviction among a smaller but significant group —a conviction which I share—that the existential approach could make a decisive and unique contribution to the future development of psychotherapy in this country. But, on the other hand, there had been much hostility, contempt and disparagement toward existentialism, particularly on the part of those psychologists and psychiatrists ensconced behind the dogmatic stockades of orthodoxy, whether Freudian, behavioristic, or other forms.

So complex, indeed, was this paradoxical relationship

that it often seemed that a good deal of the overt interest in the field on the part of psychologists and psychiatrists had been in the service of their hostility toward the ideas. They read, that is to say, in order to refute, rather than to understand. The book, *Existence: A New Dimension in Psychiatry and Psychology*, which several years ago introduced some of the works of the leading European existential psychiatrists into English for the first time, has had a relatively wide sale. But some of the interest in the book among my colleagues reminds me of an experience with a friend of mine, a young Catholic priest, whom I met on an island in Maine some twenty-five years ago, and with whom I used to go fishing. One day he noticed on the shelves in my room a number of books by Freud, whom I was then studying. He proceeded to tell me in succinct sentences just why Freud was wrong. Since this was before the time when Freud or the other psychotherapists were read in theological seminaries, either Catholic or Protestant, I wondered whether he knew much about the master of Vienna. When I asked whether he had read anything about Freud, he answered, "Oh, yes, every student in my seminary is required to read one book about him." I thought this very enlightened; and I asked what the book was. He answered that the title was *Freud Refuted.*

Our task of relating existentialism to psychology is made more difficult by the fact that only recently has the existential approach in psychiatry and psychology begun to find its particular American form and significance. When this approach was first introduced in America, the writings and speeches on existential psychotherapy were a "Tower of Babel," a confusion of tongues. There were voices which said that existential psychology was Adlerian, others that it came from Jung, others that it was all in Freud, still others that it was identical with psychodrama, and so on. These spokesmen seemed blithely unaware of their patent contradictions: if existential psychotherapy were one of these things, it could not be the others. Existential psychology was identified with Zen Buddhism and anti-intellectual trends, on one hand, or with a superintellectual philosophy composed of untranslatable German terms, on the other. It was said to be therapy which everyone does when he is doing good therapy, and also to be—especially in its classical phenomenological wing —a philosophical analysis which had nothing whatever to do with the practice of therapy as such.[1]

One purpose, or at least opportunity, which a confusion of voices lays upon us is the requirement that we cut through the faddist and bandwagon tendencies which bedevil any new movement of ideas. I shall here try to do that.[2] My purpose in this paper will be, first, to inquire into the reasons behind the paradoxical relationship of existentialism to psychotherapy. Second, to present and discuss an illustration of the relationship in the area of the problem of death. And third, to cite some criticisms and dangers in the existential emphasis in psychotherapy.

I. THE PARADOXICAL RELATION OF EXISTENTIALISM AND AMERICAN PSYCHOLOGY

The underlying affinity of American psychological thought and existentialism can be seen in the ideas of the "father" of American psychology, William James. We find

[1] I have discussed some of these problems at greater length, particularly in my book *Psychology and the Human Dilemma* (New York: Van Nostrand, 1966). My purpose in this chapter will be simply to summarize here the relevant points where a particular topic overlaps with my writings elsewhere.

[2] That the existential approach is now finding its basic form and significance in America is shown by the seminal books in the field published in the last year alone. To name a few: Erwin Straus, *Phenomenological Psychology*; Adrian Van Kaam, *Existential Foundations of Psychology*; James Bugental, *The Quest for Integrity*; Joseph Lyons, *Psychology and Phenomenology*; Clark Moustakas, *Existential Therapy with Children*.

in James a passionate emphasis on the immediacy of experience, a theme central in existentialism. We find also a belief that will and decision are prerequisite to seeing truth: you not only cannot know truth by remaining in your detached armchair, James vehemently insisted, but your very discovering of truth is in some sense dependent upon your willing, your commitment to it. His emphasis on knowing by doing (present in different forms of American pragmatism) has a familiar ring when we read Kierkegaard's existential argument that "Trust exists for the individual only as he himself produces it in action." James's epistemology, furthermore, is similar to that of Nietzsche in the first part of the *Will to Power,* where Nietzsche holds that truth is the way a biological group actualizes itself. William James was characterized by a great humanity and breadth in his own right as a person. Trained as a physician, he occupied at Harvard the chair of philosophy, and became our most influential psychologist—a cross-fertilization of disciplines which in itself is very existential.

It is not so surprising that James should sound so much like Kierkegaard, for James came back from his studies in Europe in the last decades of the nineteenth century in reaction against the same thing Kierkegaard fought, namely Hegel's pan-rationalism. Neither James nor Kierkegaard could accept Hegel's identification of truth with abstract concepts. The New Englander and the Dane, both passionate, both suffering from periodic melancholy, both possessed of dazzling capacities of spirit and brilliant literary styles, had a good deal in common in their rebellion against what they believed was the destruction of man's spirit in making abstract concepts the ultimate criteria of life.

Husserl, the father of modern phenomenology which became the first stage in the existential psychotherapeutic development, noted some decades ago the significance of James in this movement. A contemporary psychologist in

Holland, Linschoten, has made this clear. I quote from Professor Adrian Van Kaam:

> One of the leading European existential phenomenologists J. Linschoten wrote a book in 1959 *Towards a Phenomenology*, with the subtitle, *The Psychology of William James*. . . . In the introduction the diary of Husserl is quoted where the father of European phenomenology admits the influence of the thought of this great American on his own. The book shows in a well-documented way that the hidden intention of James' thinking has been realized . . . in the phenomenological-existential movement. James was groping toward a vaguely felt new phase in the history of Western mankind. Rooted in the preceding cultural period, he believed in psychology as it was practiced but he expressed continuous dissatisfaction with the exclusively one-sided approach. Linschoten concludes in his final chapter that James was on the road towards a phenomenological psychology before Butendijk, Merleau-Ponty and Straus and was already ahead of them in his concern for the integration of an objectifying psychology within the frame of a descriptive psychology.[3]

In American psychology since James, however, the emphasis on "knowing by doing" tended to become more and more knowing *only* by doing, or by what somebody else does. We found ourselves in a steadily increasing emphasis on *practice* and *behavior* and *action* to the exclusion of the total experiencing person. The criteria then became more and more those related to external behavior and those aspects of experience which would be viewed from the outside and could be measured—or at least so it seemed—objectively and in quantifiable terms. We moved toward behaviorism in psychology and toward mechanistic preoccupations in psychoanalysis. This is particularly true in the Anglo-Saxon countries: the English language is par-

[3] Adrian Van Kaam, "The Impact of Existential Phenomenology on the Psychological Literature of Western Europe," in *The Review of Existential Psychology and Psychiatry*, Vol. 1, No. 1 (Winter, 1961), pp. 68–92. The book by Professor Linschoten mentioned by Van Kaam is fortunately now being translated in English.

ticularly suited to expressing direct, concrete behavior, and not as well suited for rational and aesthetic subtlety as the French, or profound and abstruse abstractions as the German. Thus whenever psychoanalysis crossed the sea—either the English Channel or the Atlantic Ocean—it tended first to lose its deeper mythology and then to become more empirical, pragmatic, and behavioristic.

There are many socio-cultural influences in the development of American character which bear upon these points. One was the necessity of great emphasis on practice and technique in subduing the frontier. Another was great spatial motility. Since there was always some new place to go, Americans emphasized external *space* in our thinking without needing, as our European colleagues did, to go vertically into our own inner experience in the more subjective and psychological category of *time*. A third was our demonstrated success in taking our destiny into our own hands economically and materially: our economic motility, as Tillich remarks, is not only a materialism but has within it the spiritual attitude of courage to risk onself in action.

But these virtues in the American character carried with them serious dangers, and here is where the paradox of the suppression of the existential attitude becomes clearer. The emphasis on "practice" and spatial motility led to the worship of technique as a mechanical way of controlling nature, and to the corollary need therefore to see human personality as an object of control like the rest of nature. Belief in technique can be an effective anxiety-allaying method. It goes with the hope, frantic though illusory, that somehow, if we can only find the right technique, we shall not have to face the devastating anxiety of the present world predicament.

These virtues have likewise played into an overoptimism about human nature, an optimism which understandably though unfortunately became married to our faith in techniques. One of our serious dangers in America is the tendency to believe that technique *in itself* changes people, that anyone can change in any direction if only he finds the right method or the right drug. This faith is often a substitute for courage inwardly to confront one's own existence. *To do* is often easier, and may allay anxiety more quickly, than *to be*.

Thus our paradoxical situation in America is that while our underlying attitudes and temperament are highly existential, we tend to repress these under our overarching preoccupation with external behavior, techniques, and empirical forms. As partial demonstration of this paradox, William James was overlooked or held up to mild contempt in American psychology in the period between the two world wars. His *Varieties of Religious Experience* was read in religion courses, his *Will to Believe* in ethics; but so far as I can recall in psychological classes he was debunked and patronized as naïve and not "scientific" enough for us. There is no doubt that the present situation became such that, as Gustav Bergmann puts it, "virtually every American psychologist, whether he knows it or not, is nowadays a methodological behaviorist."[4] What is even more critical for our present discussion is that a three-cornered liaison tended to develop among behaviorism in psychology, orthodox Freudianism in psychoanalysis, and positivism in philosophy. An example of one side of the liaison is the great similarity between Hull's drive-reduction theory of learning and Freud's concept of pleasure, the goal of behavior, as consisting of the reduction of stimuli. An example of another

4 Quoted by Helen Sargent in a paper "Intrapsychic Change: Methodological Problems in Psychotherapy Research," in *Psychiatry: Journal for the Study of Interpersonal Processes*, Vol. 24, No. 2 (May, 1961). Dr. Sargent, disagreeing with what she calls Bergmann's arresting orthodoxy, goes on to quote Max Planck, "There is scarcely any scientific principle that is not nowadays challenged by somebody," and herself holds, "Science has more leeway than the graduate student is permitted to realize."

side of the *ménage-a-trois* is the statement of the philosopher Herman Feigl, in his address at a recent annual convention of the American Psychological Association, that Freud's specific mechanisms can be formulated and used scientifically, but such concepts as the "death instinct" cannot be.

But the important point is that such concepts as the "death instinct" in Freud were precisely what saved him from the full mechanistic implications of his system. These concepts always point beyond the deterministic limitations of his theory. They are, in the best sense of the word, a mythology. Freud was never content to let go of this mythological dimension in his thinking despite his great efforts at the same time to formulate psychology in terms of nineteenth-century biological mechanisms. In my judgment, his mythology is fundamental to the greatness of his contribution and essential to his central discoveries, such as the "unconscious." His myths are likewise essential to his radical contribution to the new image of man, namely, man as pushed by demonic, tragic, and destructive forces.

I have tried elsewhere to show that Freud's tragic concept of the Oedipus is closer to the truth than our contemporary tendency to see the Oedipus complex in terms of discrete sexual and hostile relationships in the family. The formulation of the "death instinct" as a *biological instinct* does not make sense, of course, and in this sense is rightly rejected by American behaviorism and positivism. But as a psychological and spiritual symbol of the tragic nature of man, the idea has very great importance indeed and transcends any purely biological or mechanistic interpretation.

The existential development, in modern culture known as existentialism, dealing centrally with the individual in his immediate reality as he suffers anxiety, conflict, loneliness, and as he struggles with his possibilities for love and creativity, has come to many of us as a way out of this paradox discussed above. Professor Abraham Maslow puts it excellently:

> It is extremely important for psychologists that existentialists may supply psychology with the underlying philosophy that it now lacks. Logical positivism has been a failure, especially for clinical and personality psychologists. The basic philosophical problems will surely be opened for discussion again, and perhaps psychologists will stop relying on pseudo-solutions or on unconscious, unexamined philosophies that they picked up as children.[5]

Dr. Maslow made that prediction in 1960. Since that time, his prediction has indeed become fact in several important ways. One is the formation for the first time of a division of Philosophical Psychology in the American Psychological Association. Another is the organizing of the Association of Humanistic Psychology. It is fair to say that the earlier "shock troop" work of the existential psychologists opened the way and provided some of the impetus for these developments.

We have been concerned above with the theoretical side of the paradox in America in the relation of existential ideas to psychotherapy. There is also an interesting and highly significant *practical* aspect of the same paradox which has been an important reason for the interest of many of us in the existential approach. It arises from the fact that modern Western man has succeeded all too well in making himself over into the image of a bundle of conditioned reflexes and a composite of the discrete Freudian mechanisms. But it turns out that this is precisely the source of his "neurosis"—as is demonstrated in great numbers of typical modern cases.

We rarely find outright repression of sexuality of the kind which led to Freud's original formulation of the discrete mechanisms. Contemporary man represses just the

5 Abraham H. Maslow, "Existential Psychology—What's in It for Us?" in *Existential Psychology*, ed., Rollo May (New York: Random House, 1961).

opposite needs and values, namely his sense of freedom and personal responsibility. No one needs to tell the present intelligent citizen that he is a creature of ubiquitous sexual drives, that he is largely determined by irrational psychic and economic forces over which he has little if any control, that he is an animal with an animal's instincts and destructiveness (and that while dog eats dog, *Homo sapiens* is busy proving the correctness of Oscar Wilde's line, "each man kills the thing he loves"), that his altruism and ideals are largely a reaction formation against his own inner hostility, that anxiety and guilt are morbid and lead to sickness (though how much you can get rid of them is an open question), that we marry our mothers and yearn for them to nurse us, and that we are doomed to wander through divorce courts and Alcoholics Anonymous meetings and fresh marriage rites, forever trying to make the best of our sorry fate. Indeed, these ideas—so much of a blow to our Victorian fathers' narcissism—are today not repressed by anyone who reads paperbacks or the *New York Times*. And people don't need to come to psychoanalysis to learn this —they know it all too well when they arrive.

What upsets contemporary man's security, however, is the admission of the opposite ideas and attitudes. We are afraid of (and therefore must repress), not the image of ourselves as sexual, driven creatures, but the possibility that we as individuals have freedom and responsibility, that we can choose even in our victimized state and need not be robots unless we abdicate conscious decision. We repress the awareness that we are never *just* an animal and cannot be reduced to one, that the truth we discover depends at least in part on our own commitment and much of it will not be true (such as in love and art and work) unless we bet our heart on it, that anxiety and guilt—far from being just morbid—have their normal and constructive side and are necessary concomitants to creativity, and that we are not just the "sports" of evolution but that the essential character of the human being is his capacity to choose and affirm values which have more significance for him than even his own survival.

If my rhetoric seems rash, let me hasten to add that we can demonstrate every hour of the day in our clinical work in psychoanalysis the truth of these contentions. Nowadays in our work with patients we find that *tenderness* tends to be repressed more than sexuality. It used to be the hope of people in the Victorian day that they could be in love without falling into sex; now they hope that they can have sex without falling into love. *Trust* is experienced by our typical contemporary patient in psychoanalysis as more dangerous than hostility or suspicion, generosity as more anxiety-creating than selfish calculation.[6]

Now the existentialist emphases lead us to view the evasion and repression of tenderness, closeness, commitment, decision, and trust as aspects of the individual's running away from his human situation and his being. Gabriel Marcel speaks trenchantly of modern man's repression of "the sense of the ontological—the sense of being." "Indeed I wonder," he writes, "if a psychoanalytic method, deeper and more discerning than any that has been evolved until now, would not reveal the morbid effects of the repression of this sense and of the ignoring of this need."[7]

Similarly Professor Michael Wyschogrod states in his discussion of Heidegger, "This state of ontological uprootedness is the particular malady of modern man whose technological reason is a splendid example of the extent to which humanly constructed forms can obstruct that recep-

6 Those who wish clinical data on the difficulty of trust for modern patients will find it in an interesting and useful paper, "The Existential Moment in Psychotherapy," by Pieter C. Kors, in *Psychiatry: Journal for the Study of Interpersonal Processes*, Vol. 24, No. 2 (May, 1961), pp. 153–163.

7 Gabriel Marcel, *The Philosophy of Existence* (New York: Philosophical Library, 1949), p. 1.

tive attitude to being to which Heidegger wishes to return."[8]

II. THE PROBLEM OF DEATH

We shall now apply the existential approach in psychology to the problem of death. Death has been one of the "taboo" topics in psychology—along with extrasensory perception, homosexuality (until recently), and even existentialism itself in some quarters. These taboo topics have one thing in common: to take them seriously would be to threaten widely and deeply entrenched biases in our cultural beliefs and our scientific methods.

It is not, thus, by accident that a paper on death was included in the first symposium on existential psychology at the annual convention of the American Psychological Association.[9] The existential approach opens up significant new areas for inquiry: this role of "gadfly" to entrenched biases is one of its genuine contributions. Thus the topic of death is useful for our inquiring into the interrelation of the existential approach with psychology.

Heidegger, the existentialist who talks most about death, has held that death is the one absolute fact, the only final and certain fact in anyone's life. Thus, said Heidegger, death individualizes man. I do not think Heidegger ever read the psychologist Otto Rank, but Rank also expressed the belief that death confirms man's individualization. My death means something qualitatively different to me from what it can mean to you, and vice versa. No one can die for me; the anticipation of my own death is what cuts me off and makes me stand alone.[10]

---

8 Michael Wyschogrod, *Existential Psychoanalysis* (lecture, to be published).

9 In 1959.

10 Writes Heidegger, "Death is an irrelative potentiality which singles man out and individualizes him to make him understand the potentiality of being in others as well as himself, when he realizes the inescapable nature of his own death."

1. *The Repression of Death*

When we try to orient ourselves to the topic of death, we are struck immediately by one phenomenon. This is that modern Western civilization, particularly in America, has made a fetish of the *repression of death*. As in Victorian times sex was repressed, so now death and its symbolism are repressed.[11] Death is obscene, unmentionable, pornographic,

11 See the studies of death and death symbolism in Hiroshima by the psychiatrist Robert Jay Lifton.

not to be looked at if one can help it, not to be talked about in polite company. We have big funeral services which seem purposed to demonstrate that, after all, the person did not die. We buy "life insurance" which, despite its euphemistic name doesn't insure life at all, but simply enables our heirs to be less economically burdened by our decease. Their life can go on—ironically through *our* life insurance—as though we hadn't died. Death is viewed—again like sex by the nice Victorian woman—as a dirty mistake, an unfortunate plague on our universe, perhaps necessary as nature's way of getting rid of the population our sexuality spawns, but to be ignored as much as possible.

As a result we look upon grief and mourning as sick. The implication is that, when someone dies, it is better if you don't feel grief, or at least the less the better; which means, in a strange kind of logic, the more you deny the fact of death, the "healthier" you are.

When individuals and social groups consistently repress and deny an experience which is both powerful and real, as Freud rightly demonstrated with sexuality, some symptoms are bound to appear. In my judgment the repression of death produces the symptoms of lack of zest, lack of experience of oneself as alive and vital, and the kind of depression in which one experiences himself as a creature of mechanical action. Repression of death tends to make life banal, empty, vapid.

Entwined in this repression is the romantic conviction

that somehow life goes on and on and on. Our culture runs away from death by making a cult of everlasting progress, which is bound to become utopian. Utopianism seems to me to be a reaction formation to our despair in facing death, by which we keep the repression going. When I listen to speeches from Washington about the Great Society, for example, I am particularly dismayed by the fact that almost all the words are comparatives. I hear that we will live longer and healthier, more people will travel farther by the new trains and we'll go faster in the air, more money will be earned, more automobiles built, we'll all be richer and richer. This "er"—the comparative—seems to have become the ultimate symbol of the perpetual motion of progress.

All of this is predicated on the assumption that the meaning of life is simply how much longer we can live. We slide into the illusion that death is outwitted by the fact that we can prolong life a few more years (often, of course, into a lingering old age marked by invalidism, debility, senility, and loneliness). The ironic result is a denial not only of the reality of life but a source of the banality of our day-to-day experience.

There is also in the repression of death a source of some of the curious perversions that appear in odd ways in modern society. Geoffrey Gorer, who has been an astute commentator on American civilization, thinks that in this denial of death lies the root of the violence and sadism that comes out in American comics and television programs. Noting the repression of the topic of death as pornographic, Gorer goes on:

> Nevertheless, people have to come to terms with the basic facts of birth, copulation and death, and somehow accept their implications; if social prudery prevents this being done in an open and dignified fashion, then it will be done surreptitiously. If we dislike the modern pornography of death, then we must give back to death—natural death—its parade and publicity, re-admit grief and mourning. If we make death unmentionable in polite society

—'not in front of the children'—we almost insure continuation of the 'horror comic.' No censorship has ever been really effective.[12]

Unfortunately the Christian misuse of hope has played into the American romantic illusion that we somehow can escape death. The Jesuit writer Father William Lynch has noted this perversion:

> What follows for the imagination if it does not have the elementary gift of dealing *directly* with the image and fact of death? It will then deal with it indirectly, that is to say, in bizarre ways. . . . Its usual formula is violence. The violent and sadistic imagination, therefore, rather than indicating strength and masculinity, signifies the evasion of a fact. The imagination must be a coping, not an evading, instrument.[13]

Mourning, indeed, is psychologically an exceedingly necessary and healthy function. If somebody we love dies, crying and sadness are not only cathartic, but they are the ways of giving up our dependency, shifting our love for the lost one to inner meanings and memories where it can stay with us, and relocating and redirecting our own attachments. Similarly, if something dies in oneself—say an ambition dies, a plan in which we invested great hope—the constructive way to face the loss is the way of grief.[14]

This romanticization is a new, and to me the most harmful, form of the American dream. It is the dream that in prin-

12 Geoffrey Gorer, "The Pornography of Death," in *The Berkley Book of Modern Writing*, #3, edited by William Phillips and Philip Rahv (New York: Berkeley Publishing Corp., 1956) , p. 62.

13 William F. Lynch, *Images of Hope* (Baltimore: Helicon Press, 1965), p. 245.

14 It seems to me a curious misuse of religion that we protect ourselves from grief on the basis of the belief, for example, that Christianity has "transcended death." I propose that it is a prostitution of the doctrine of the Christian resurrection to believe that religious convictions of any sort can be employed as a means of detouring around the fact of death. The meaning of religion which we can achieve requires the courageous mourning and experiencing of the grief that comes from directly confronting the reality of death.

ciple we need never die—or if *we* do die, at least our descen-
dants will live on in a world of such great progress medically
and psychologically that *they* shall never die. Since, however,
we still know we do die, what we have to do is repress the
significance of death in order to cling to our assumption that
life goes on perpetually. This goes hand in hand with the
glorification of youth, and ironically and paradoxically, we
have lost any place for the wisdom of old age.

2. *Erich Fromm: Biophilia and Necrophilia*

The repression of death and the symbols of death are not
absent among psychologists. We shall cite here as an example
a book by Erich Fromm, *The Heart of Man*. Here Fromm
separates people into two categories: those who love life—
this type he calls the "biophilous"—and those who love death,
the "necrophilous." These latter, of which Hitler is a "pure
example," are characterized by their preoccupation with
faeces, decay, and destruction. "Man's aim in life," Fromm
states, "is to be attracted by all that is alive and separate himself from all that is dead and mechanical."[15] Man should
look at, concern himself with, "love" all things related to life,
and should think of nothing less than death.

Many of Fromm's statements, whether they are entirely
adequate or not, no one would quarrel with, such as "Good
is all that serves life" and "Evil is all that serves death."[16]
But they are *formed into a system which makes death itself
the evil to be avoided*. And, since we can not avoid the fact
that we shall die, the implication is that we not look at it,
and in effect evade a large segment of the reality of our
human experience.

This dichotomy gets Fromm into curious contradictions
and leads us to ask a number of questions. In setting necro-

[15] Erich Fromm, *The Heart of Man* (New York: Harper & Row, 1964),
p. 48.

[16] *Ibid.*, p. 47.

philia and biophilia up as the diametric extremes, Fromm
seems to equate the former with psychosis. "The pure necrophile is insane,"[17] he says; and again, "necrophilia is insani-
ty." Several things need to be said about this. First, a concept
from psychopathology (the term necrophilia is in origin the
term for the morbid symptom of desiring to have intercourse
with someone's dead body) cannot be carried over as a norm
for human beings in general.[18] But an even more serious
point arises. Does Fromm not cruelly mistake the nature of
mental illness? The insane are surely not those who "love
death"! They are, rather, those who have experienced such
unfortunate circumstances (outward and inward) in life at
an age or condition in which they could not adequately react,
that they have had radically to shrink their lives to avoid
entire destruction; their hard struggle is to avoid death and
still preserve a little life.

Another contradiction lies in Fromm's relating his necrophilia to the "anal character" in classical psychoanalysis. He
states that one way children get started "loving death" is that
their parents put too much emphasis on faeces, and the child
thus learns to be too concerned with faeces, decay, and dead
things. But actually is not the source of the anal character
just the opposite, namely, the pattern in which Victorian
parents repress concern with faeces, are too squeamish to see
and deal with excrement, afraid to affirm the child's pleasure
in his faeces, and institute rigid training so that toilet concerns can be suppressed out of awareness? It is a truism these
days that some pleasure and satisfaction in his faeces is a
normal and healthy thing for the child, and is one source of
later creativity.

Another strange result of Fromm's separating of the
"sheep" from the "goats" is seen in his naming Carl Jung
as an "outstanding example" of the "necrophilous character."

[17] *Ibid.*, p. 48.
[18] This was Paul Tillich's criticism of this paper of Fromm's.

He cites Jung's interest in the corpse of a French soldier who
had apparently been killed a century and a half earlier, which
was unearthed during the excavation of his house, and Jung's
general interest in death as shown in his dreams and conversation. But the curious fact is that, among the early group
of leaders in the psychoanalytic field—Freud, Adler, Jung,
Rank, et al.—Jung was the one who *did* love life, was robust
and lived with a good deal of zest, sexually and otherwise.
Whether we advocate this and whether we agree with Jung's
theories are of course entirely separate questions. But the
simple fact seems to be that Jung, in sharp contrast to most
others in the psychoanalytic field, lived a "happy life."[19]

After a long and vivid page quoting things purporting
to show that Jung was necrophiliac, Fromm adds that Jung
was "an unusually creative person," and "creation is the opposite to necrophilia." The explanation, Fromm says, is that
Jung solved his conflict by balancing his destructive forces
against his constructive ones. But far from this being an in-
cidental point, as Fromm makes it, isn't it the basic point all
along—that creativity and other positive goals of life come
not out of "biophilia" as the opposite to "necrophilia," but
exactly out of the dialectic relation between the two? As Tillich and Goldstein would put it, creativity comes from the
struggle of being against nonbeing. Creativity is born in the
confronting of death.

Perhaps the most serious contradiction of all in Fromm's
thesis is his citing, as his "most excellent" example of what
he means by biophilia, of the Spanish philosopher Unamuno.
At the beginning of the Spanish Civil War, during a speech
by the Fascist General Millan Astray on taking over the
University of Salamanca where Unamuno had been rector,
the General cried, "Long live death!" Unamuno, then a man
of eighty, made a heroic speech not unlike Socrates' *Apologia*,

[19] Gerald Sykes, *The Hidden Remnant* (New York: Harper & Row, 1962).

in which he concluded, "This is the temple of the intellect. I am its high priest." And admitting that they, the Falanges, would win because of their brute strength, he took his stand still with "Reason and Right."

But Fromm seems to have no awareness that this is the Unamuno who wrote *The Tragic Sense of Life* and who could take such a heroic stand precisely because he spent his life concerned about tragedy, facing evil directly, not looking away from death, Unamuno, along with Ortega y Gasset, is representative of the existential movement as it came into Spain; he spent his life "shaping paradoxes," as he proclaimed in the speech referred to above.

What we miss entirely in Fromm is this sense of the tragic. The chief problem is that such a dichotomy as Fromm makes leads inescapably, quite apart from any intention of the author's, to playing ostrich with evil and tragedy.[20] Fromm says that when some people see their own necrophiliac elements, they are "shocked by how close they were to the valley of the shadow of death,"[21] and this may make them hurry over to the side of life. At another point he speaks of the "valley of the shadow of death" as something to be avoided like the plague.[22] The psalmist, however, took a very different view. He faced death directly as part of the human situation, "*Though* I walk through the valley of the shadow of death, I will fear no evil, for thou art with me."

This brings us to another methodological confusion in Fromm's chapter on death, and that is the confusing of religious and psychological categories. "The pure necrophile is insane; the pure biophile is saintly."[23] Fromm holds that the

20 Was not the optimistic, romantic liberalism in America one of the chief reasons Americans did not take Hitler seriously at first? Americans had so much suppressed their awareness of the degree of possible human evil that they could not believe he was as bad as reported.

21 *Ibid.*, p. 48.

22 *Ibid.*, p. 59.

23 *Ibid.*, p. 48.

necrophile and the biophile are diametric opposites. But obviously "insane" and "saintly" are not opposites, but are on different levels. Many saintly persons, like creative geniuses, would be closer technically to the "insane" if you must use psycho-diagnostic categories; their genius, whether in art or religion, is not purchased cheaply. By the same token, Fromm cites Albert Schweitzer as one of the "great representatives of the love of life."[24] But Schweitzer speaks not of "love of life" but of "*reverence* for life," which in him comes out of a very specific religious tradition and source. Surely this means something quite different from "biophilia."[25]

One other curious but consistent result of this dichotomy is that we come in Fromm to the emphasis on sadness as bad. "Sadness is sinful," says Fromm at one point,[26] and again, "sadness is sin."[27] But is not sadness a very healthy and necessary emotion when someone or something we love dies, or when there is a tragic conflict? Grief and mourning have similarly a necessary and useful function. Many of us are profoundly sad about social and political injustice and cruelty in our world, and I am sure Dr. Fromm is also; and this sadness normally can and should be motivation for positive action against the evils in the situation.

These strictures against sadness come close to supporting exactly what Fromm once so eloquently attacked, namely the "Brave New World." In his recent books, Fromm is writing in the philosophical area of vitalism, as for example in Bergson and Nietzsche, but without the dialectical thought which gave depth to Bergson, and without the tragic sense

24 *Ibid.*, p. 47.

25 Fromm quotes as support for his thesis Spinoza's statement, "Everything in so far as it is itself, endeavors to persist in its own being." The term "being" should not be identified, as Fromm does, with biological *life*. To persist in what one conceives of as his being may require, as it did with Jesus and Socrates, giving up one's life.

26 *Ibid.*, p. 47.

27 *Ibid.*, p. 48.

which saved Nietzsche from simple naturalism. There has been an increasing element of utopianism in Fromm's work since *The Sane Society*. Utopianism can be understandably viewed as an endeavor, whether through faith in automatic progress of new forms of production or sheer fantasy, to escape the inevitability of death. The more profound elements in Fromm's thought, which made his early books, particularly *Escape from Freedom*, so significant and influential, are unfortunately now largely absent in his writings—a phenomenon about which one can have genuine and appropriate sadness indeed.

Fromm finally in this book discusses modern man's infatuation with "mechanisms" and the nuclear war preparations, topics on which he has always been cogent and persuasive. But again, his new dichotomy leads him seriously astray. He questions why people accept the vast preparations for nuclear war so docilely and with so little protest, and gives the answer, because they "love death." I propose the exact opposite, namely, that their apathy is related to the *repression* of the reality of death. We don't look at death, we believe somehow a holocaust "can't happen here," and so go on trusting that since civilization survived gunpowder and the bow and arrow, it will survive the nuclear bomb.

We have already noted that Geoffrey Gorer holds that we have such preoccupation with violence and sadism not because we think of death but *because we repress death* and its symbols, because we think of it as obscene, sick. And the return of the repressed in this case is sadism and violence.

What is wholly omitted by Fromm is the fact that those who truly are devoted to life are able to be so by virtue of confronting death. The loving of life *for its own sake* is a dehumanization of the human being. Fromm notes with commendation that "man will do almost anything to preserve his life."[28] True; and this has been universally recognized as the most craven aspect of man. The human being

28 *Ibid.*, p. 45.

is distinguished in the evolutionary line by virtue of the fact that he has the potentiality for just the opposite: he can hold some values more important to him than life itself. "Give me liberty or give me death," is not mere histrionics or to be dismissed as neurotic. It can be an authentic expression of the human being acting at his noblest and most fully human level. If the mere fact of perpetuating life is the ultimate goal, we have to some extent lost the distinguishing qualities of being human. All through history, except possibly since the great triumph of our industrial age, men have known that unless they were willing to die for something, their lives would be empty. The Greeks said in a hundred different ways that unless one has the courage to give up his life for some value, life itself will have no meaning. "Not life is to be valued," said Aristotle, "but the *good* life."

When biological life itself is the ultimate value—which I have characterized as a deterioration of the American dream—one must hang on at all costs, and what results is a kind of death-in-life, that is, conformism. Conformism is the tendency of the individual to let himself be swallowed up in a sea of collective responses and attitudes. It is the loss of his own awareness, the loss of his potentialities and sensibilities, the loss of whatever characterizes him as a unique being. By this means he temporarily escapes the anxiety of death, the anxiety of "nonbeing," but at the price of forfeiting life, surendering his own possibilities and sense of existence. As Paul Tillich put it, he gives up *being* because he is afraid of *nonbeing*. It is a surrendering of the meaning of life because he is afraid of death.

The relation of creativity to death is important at this point. Biological analogies abound: a simple one is the baby teeth being pushed out to make room for the adult teeth. A psychological analogy is the adolescent's need to fight his parents (which he typically has to do with overdone force) to become free to find a partner of his own to love outside the family. Every original thought and idea I achieve requires that something in my old way of thinking die. This is why artists and poets are always telling us that the recognition of death is essential to the creative act, and that the creative act itself, from birth on, is the capacity to die in order that something new may be born.

A work of art, I am suggesting, is born in the destruction of one form in order that a new form may be created. My security is always to greater or less degree threatened in this destruction of my old accustomed forms, my familiar ways of thinking. The anxiety that the creative person must face is the anxiety of nothingness, the anxiety of the abyss, which occurs in the process of the destruction of the old as something new is born.

The sexual orgasm—which is one aspect of biological creativity—is symbolically related in many kinds of mythology to an act of death. It is necessary to be able to surrender oneself to the greater biological purpose, which is shown in the examples of the bee and the praying mantis. The act of copulation also is in some mythology and language synonymous with death. During the Renaissance the pun *amore* (love) and *more* (death) was rampant in the literature—which implies something significant psychologically even if the roots of the words are quite separate. Fortunately for us human beings, literal death does not occur each time we make love, but something of that quality does occur; we cannot love unless we can let ourselves go, abandon ourselves, give ourselves over to a self-transcending process which shakes our previous security to the very roots.

There is a significant relationship, I suggest, between the repression of death in our day and the fact that sexual activity—which in our heyday of liberalism is no longer repressed at all—tends to be an empty, technical performance, without strong feeling or passion. When sex becomes a mechanical means by which one releases tension in a simulated relatedness, its clinical reason is not infrequently the fear of the genuine intimacy required for the birth of new relationship between the two people. If we are unwilling or unable to face partial deaths, we cling to the familiar or to the family. We go through life always symbolically hanging on to an uncut umbilical cord. This surrender of originality is both cause and effect of the staleness of human experience and the "deadness" of our actual life.

3. Death and the Consciousness of Being

The essential characteristic of the death-in-life which we have been describing is the *diminishing of the person's own consciousness*. The critical issue in the facing of death lies in this area of the human being's capacity for self-consciousness.[29] This is true not only in the respect that actual death consists of the blotting out of consciousness, but in the respect that the *experience* of being alive, in contrast to mere *biological* existence, lies in certain qualities of consciousness. My consciousness is what is unique about me; I experience my ideas in a way nobody else does. My feelings, my tastes— to the extent I can be honest with myself—are to some significant extent different from the next person's; my perception, my way of seeing any given scene has a unique original form.[30] My values, if they are worth anything, will be values

[29] I am not talking about facing death by physically courting it; such behavior as rash speeding on a motorcycle is well known to be an expression of one's own doubts of one's courage. The "hot flyers" who take rash chances in war are compensating for anxiety. (Cf. Rollo May, *Meaning of Anxiety*).

[30] Back in my artist days, I noticed that when a group of us was painting a model, each one of us perceived the model differently; she was a genuinely different figure to me from what she was to the painter next to me. This was not because one of us was a better artist than the other. Nor would it make any sense whatever to aver, "We shall measure this woman to see whether she is the way *I* am painting her or *you* are." The point is, rather, that human consciousness, by virtue of its being the consciousness of a unique individual, is such that the form of life which is perceived by that consciousness has to have uniqueness. This is the richness, the sensitivity, the greatness—and also the terror—of each individual act of conciousness.

the original affirmation of which begin with this original act of consciousness. Thus, as we consider now the constructive approach to the problem of death, we shall find the question of relating to the fact of death in each individual's own consciousness the center of our inquiry.

The human being is differentiated from the rest of evolution by the fact that he can, and in some way must, anticipate his own death. We know that we die; we have a word for death. This makes death the most "personal" thing in the ultimate sense. This very personal nature of the experience is related, via repression, to our need to make death impersonal. We obscure death by resorting to statistics. We state that "one" dies, rather than that "I" die, hiding the fact that the real problem for me, as for any man, is that at some moment in some actual day *my* life will end. If it sounds like a truism, it is a highly provocative and helpful one, that the mere courageous awareness of the fact I will die is not only the first stage in constructively meeting the problem, but also is in itself an ennobling act.[31]

The awareness of death sharpens our sense of being. This sounds paradoxical, but I am not using words loosely. The capacity to face death is the means by which we gain freedom. Man is the being who knows that at some future moment he will not be; he always is in a dialectical relationship with his own death. In the face of this, he may repress

31 Blaise Pascal here has a penetrating observation: "Man is only a reed, the feeblest thing in nature; but he is a thinking reed. There is no need for the entire universe to arm itself in order to annihilate him: a vapor, a drop of water, suffices to kill him. But were the universe to crush him, man would yet be more noble than that which slays him, because he knows that he dies, and the advantage that the universe has over him; of this the universe knows nothing. Thus all our dignity lies in thought."

By thought Pascal does not mean intellectualization or rationalization or abstract concepts, but rather the "consciousness" of which we have spoken, the "reasons of the heart" as well as the "reasons of the mind." Thus our dignity lies in consciousness, and he goes on, "By thought we raise ourselves, not by space and time, which we cannot fill. . . . Let us strive then to think well. Therein lies the principle of morality."

what he "knows," thus cutting off his being—which is what is meant by conformity, by giving up his ideas to fit into the group and becoming an organization man, by adjusting, by surrendering his consciousness. But there is the other alternative. If I can know that at any moment I am on the edge of possible annihilation, then existence becomes something that is not automatic; experience loses its vapidness and emptiness and becomes an experience of concrete self-awareness. It takes on vitality and immediacy: I experience a heightened consciousness of myself and a heightened consciousness of the world around me. This is a sharpening of the experience of my being at this moment.

Now that is not at all to say this will be *pleasurable* or *happy consciousness*. It may well be an experience chiefly of anxiety; or, if the person has not lived with any fullness up to that point, despair. No one escapes the fear of death. To "want" to die may be the gift of the martyrs, but when any-one who is not in that state claims he wants to die, or does not fear death, I suspect some repressions or skull-duggery with words. But by facing the unavoidable and ultimate anx-iety, at least we do not sleep our lives out, or waste our days in running from that inevitable moment of loneliness on our deathbeds. And, painful as that awareness may be, it at least does open up for us the choice of what we shall do with the hours between now and then. Thus we can take steps to bring some meaning, some love, some pleasure—some creativity—into the time which we do have.

The awareness of death is also the ultimate source of hu-man humility. The fact that we all at some time will die puts every man in the same boat with every other human being, free or enslaved, male or female, child or adult. Thus the facing of death is the strongest motive and requirement that we be *fellow* men: no matter how much we may dislike the Russians or the Chinese, we know that we and they will die and therefore in the last analysis, our fate will turn out the same. This is what Theseus, the hero in Sophocles' *Oedipus in Colonus,* is saying: "I know I am only a man, and I have no more to hope for in the end than you have." Death is the humanizing fact which makes us fellow men, black or white, brown or red, intelligent or stupid. It puts us beyond self-righteousness,[32] places us all in need of mercy and forgiveness by the others, and makes us participate in the human drama in which no man can stand above another.

Let us pause here to indicate a frequent detour which comes up in psychotherapeutic work. When people have recognized the fact of death, they often embark on frantic experience which they confuse with the facing of death—a pattern made famous as the "eat, drink and be merry for to-morrow you die" philosophy. Clinically we find this often in men and women in their fifties and sixties. They must do everything, go every place, love everybody—as though obsessed with hurry to wake up and live intensely before it is too late. This reminds me of the poster from a beautician's window which my students brought to me with the gleeful claim that it was the last word in existentialism, "If you have only one life to live, live it as a Clairol blonde." A great deal of the compulsive dedication to making money in our society, to living it up in the obsessional conformism of the squirrel-cage, is motivated by the individual's dread that if he were quiet, he would not be able longer to push aside the awareness that he will die.[33]

What needs to be seen in psychotherapy is that intensity of life is not necessarily correlated with *action.* Intensity consists not of how much or how fast we do things, common illusion though this be. Indeed, this very multiplying of ac-

---

[32] "God maketh his sun to shine on the just and the unjust," and by the same token, nature "maketh" us to die whether we are good or bad.

[33] Ibsen's *Peer Gynt* is a powerful portrayal of an individual compulsively running around the earth to escape recognition of the fact that he will die. I discuss this drama in detail in my book *Love and Will* (New York: W. W. Norton, 1968).

tivity may serve to dull the experiencing: eating two steaks may give less pleasure than one. Intensity, rather, consists in how much the experience affects us, how much meaning it has; and these dimensions refer to the profundity and wholeness of the experience. Profundity in turn is very much bound up with the capacity for repose, for tranquility, in which we can let the experience speak to us.

Another constructive stage in confronting death is the developing by the individual of values which are more important to him than life or death. As I have said, the characteristic that distinguishes man as human is that he holds certain values more important than life itself. Tom, the fifty-five-year-old uneducated Irishman, a typical lower-middle-class laborer, whose gastric functions were studied at New York Hospital, said after his night of greatest anxiety, "If I could not support my family, I'd as soon jump off the end of the dock."[34] He is telling us that for him life is not the value in itself, but life with the middle-class self-respect found in supporting his family. This is not chiefly an economic question; Tom could have got along on relief. What is important is his particular image of himself as a man. You may not regard Tom's lower-middle-class value as the highest possible in life, but it is at least a value that suffices to enable him to confront the idea of death, and to see that life has meaning only in terms of values which give it significance.

Let us now raise the issue of self-consciousness and death to a higher dimension by discussing the close relationship between anxiety and death. First, some definitions. I define anxiety as the individual's apprehension at a threat to values which he identifies with his existence as a self.[35] The way to meet and deal with anxiety is to identify one's existence with values that are stronger than the particular threat. The ulti-

[34] Cf. Rollo May, *The Meaning of Anxiety* (New York: Ronald Press, 1950).
[35] *Ibid.*

mate threat causing anxiety is, of course, death. The only way to meet the anxiety of death in the long run is to have values that are stronger than the fact of death. The individual's problem, therefore, becomes the developing of values that will be more significant for him than the fact of death, which may vary from Tom's self-respecting wage-earner to patriotism to love of one's children or devotion to freedom or to truth or to God. My important consideration at the moment is not the content but the function of the value. There is an inverse relationship between the soundness and strength of one's values and anxiety, especially anxiety in respect to death.[36] The firmer, the more flexible, the more profound the person's values, the more he will be able to meet anxiety in general, and the anxiety of death in particular.

I shall end this discussion despite the fact that a great deal, indeed some of the most important aspects of the confronting of death, have yet to be discussed. My purpose here is only to demonstrate, with the theme of death, how a topic which the existentialists have, in contrast to other cultural movements, discussed centrally and openly, is also important psychotherapeutically.

Since I have been arguing the personal nature of death, I may be permitted to close on a more personal tone. The question is asked so often as to become a perdurable symbol: At the time of our deaths, what will we have to account to ourselves for, what will be expected of us? In Henrik Ibsen's last play, *When We Dead Awake*, the chief character, an elderly successful sculptor who is fed up with life, asks the

[36] While I emphasize the *function* of the value, I do not mean to imply that the *content* is unimportant. Trying to overcome fear of death by manipulative values is common enough—i.e., by projecting oneself on one's children and seeking to gain immortality by controlling them from the grave, as Dr. Shinn points out to me. The dogmatic belief that God will take care of me and therefore I need not face death is using a religious content in the same way. I would regard these as "unsound" values in my terms above.

woman who was once his model and who loved him but whom he would not permit himself to love, "When we dead awaken, what shall we find?" She responds, "We shall find that we have never lived." This is one answer, and the one which haunts the days and nights of multitudes of people in our prosperous twentieth century; it generally leads them to repress even the question of death.

There are, however, other answers. Some of them may be, we have tried to know our potentialities, and to some extent at least, we have lived them out. We shall know that we have loved, and that we have made a few friends who matter to us. We shall know that we have brought some beauty and meaning into our lives. We have sought not to betray our own consciousness; and when we have betrayed it, we have let ourselves know that we have. We have not turned a deaf ear to being, but we have listened to its call, and we have responded. What more can be expected from any man?

III. SOME CRITICISMS AND CAUTIONS

After noting the relevance of existentialism to psychotherapy in one area, we turn now to a critical appraisal of some aspects of existential psychotherapy. To do so we shall look first at some comments by intelligent nonprofessional critics, for they often have had a clearer and sounder idea of the significance of existential analysis than the professional practitioners of different schools who have their own dogma to defend. Gilbert Cant, medical editor of *Time*, has in two articles, one a feature article on existential psychotherapy and the other a cover story entitled "Guilt and Anxiety," shown keen insight into the importance of the existential influence in psychotherapy as bringing back the human *being* into psychoanalysis.[37] In a less widely read but equally serious and thoughtful survey of the different psychoanalytic schools,

[37] *Time*, Dec. 29, 1958, Vol. LXXII, No. 26, and March 31, 1961, Vol. LXXVII, No. 14.

Brock Brower presents some penetrating insights into both the positive and the negative aspects of the development.

> Existential psychoanalysis [writes Brower] has certainly been the most exciting and controversial development in analysis in the last decade, though perhaps, as Dr. May sometimes thinks, there should be no movement at all, since existential analysis really only asks a new *orientation* for the analyst rather than any adherence to a new *system*. That is, that the analyst recognize a sense of being in the patient on the couch, and not let psychoanalysis become yet another of the 'new representations of the fragmentation of man.' But such statements are already a sharp criticism of the techniques of ego psychology. For if, as Dr. May writes, the analyst is now faced with patients who are lacking in affect, tending toward depersonalization, and covering up their problems by means of intellectualization and technical formulations, how can they possibly be helped by an analyst who remains depersonalized himself and offers intellectualizations and technical formulations as answers to their problems?

Mr. Brower summarizes how he believes this approach gives the breakthrough for this dilemma, and then adds significantly:

> Unfortunately the promise and excitement contained within these insights have already somewhat faded. The attacks on existential analysis as "mysticism" or "an attempt to detour" have not been half as damaging as "the tangential, screwy people who've attached themselves to it." . . . Perhaps a better way to view existential analysis is not as a movement, but as a highly structured and persistent question. It comes upon the scene just when psychoanalysis is under attack from a number of outside critics—who are no longer incensed, as in the Twenties, by its challenge to traditional values, but rather by the boredom and sterility of the current Freudian ethic it helped create—and possibly at the core of existential analysis lie the very self-doubts that many analysts must feel as this new attack mounts.[38]

Brower is right that the promise and excitement have already somewhat faded. I think this is all to the good since

[38] *Esquire,* July, 1961, Vol. LVI, No. 1, pp. 78–89.

it frees us to think more incisively and calmly about the long-term relationship of existentialism and psychotherapy. Gerald Sykes summarizes existential psychotherapy in a chapter in *The Hidden Remnant,* with the conclusion that it is "very much a step in the right direction."[39] But he adds that I, as the "perhaps too persuasive advocate" of these ideas, was naïve in that I did not realize how counter these ideas went to the American extravert dedication to the Organization Man and Madison Avenue economic success.

Sykes also is partly justified in this criticism. The first chapters in *Existence* were written noncritically, on the assumption that when someone presents a new point of view it will be accepted for what it is worth and rejected for what it is not worth. As I look back, somewhat sadder and wiser, I find my original assumption oddly *un*existential. I did not adequately foresee either the overenthusiastic bandwagon tendencies of some adherents to these ideas, on the one hand, or the unenlightened and enraged criticism of the orthodox dogmatic schools, on the other. A less naïve approach on my part would probably have reduced both of these obscurantist reactions.

I shall here cite some negative trends in the relationship of existentialism and psychotherapy which, at least in my judgment, are harmful for its future contribution.

A first harmful trend is the antiscientific, anti-intellectual tendency in some existential psychotherapy. Certainly one of the abuses to which the existential philosophical movement in Europe fell unhappy heir, despite the sophistication of Sartre and Heidegger themselves, was antirational tendencies; and the danger is even greater in America both because of the great worship of technical reason and science and the concomitant reaction against it. The fact that many thoughtful psychiatrists and psychologists and other intelligent people in our culture recognize the inadequacies of

[39] New York: Harper & Row, 1962.

present scientific methods for the study of man should lead us not to reject science as such but to seek new scientific methods which will be more adequate for revealing the nature of man.

The same with anti-intellectualism. The existential approach, however, is not rationalistic *or* antirationalistic; it is a seeking for the underlying ground in human experience in which both reason and unreason are based. Both Kierkegaard and Nietzsche knew that "man cannot sink back into unreflective immediacy without losing himself," says Karl Jaspers, "but he can go this way to the end, not destroying reflection, but rather coming to the basis in himself in which reflection is rooted."[40]

Thus the critics of existential ideas in psychiatry are right when they charge that this approach can be misused to open up the way for all kinds of "wild" statements about human beings and psychotherapy. It is one thing for Sartre to make his epigrammatic statement, "Man is a useless passion," on the basis of a profound and subtle philosophy which has great meaning and importance whether one agrees with it or not. It is quite another to out-Sartre Sartre in throwing logical essences out the window, as some writers in existential psychiatry do, disregarding the structure of reason in a way of which Sartre himself, profound and keen thinker that he is, would never have been guilty. We must not be "mis-ologists," Socrates cautions. But as existentialists we should seek to help "logos" to be given flesh.

A related problem in existential psychotherapy arises in the use of "transcendence" and similar terms as a way actually of bypassing existential experiences. One paper on "Transcendence and Healing," for example, lists the following eleven forms of transcendence in the therapeutic process: "Transcendence of the subject-object dichotomy between therapist, transcendence of the body-mind dichotomy, tran-

[40] *Reason and Existence* (New York: Noonday Press, 1955), Ch. 1.

scendence of dualistic thought, transcendence of the ego, transcendence of disease as expression of the pleasure-pain duality, transcendence of causal and teleological thinking, transcendence of the motivational split of means and ends, transcendence of the temporo-spatial coordinates of experience, transcendence of the epistemic barrier between mind and world, transcendence of the duality of being and non-being, transcendence of the separation between man and Ultimate Reality (God)."

What happens in such an approach is that practically all the age-old problems of human existence, with which thinkers have struggled since human consciousness was born, are blithely bypassed by a word. It is argued that in this "transcendence of dualistic thought," for example, the therapist uses a mode of thinking that is "beyond language and symbolic imagery," that he is freed from concepts which hamper "the capacity to see what really is," and that in such "moments of understanding there is no understander." But it is manifestly impossible to use a mode of thought that goes beyond symbolic imagery. Symbols, language of one form or another, are always the very form and content of any thinking. This error likewise has its roots in a misapplication of phenomenology. Husserl's phenomenological approach is assumed to mean that the psychotherapist observes a patient without any concepts presupposed in his own mind at all. But if you did not presuppose some concept, you would not even *perceive* what is there.

Obviously there must be an "understander" if there is to be understanding. The psychotherapist had best realize that he is seeing the patient through his own eyes and understanding the patient in his own way, which will always be limited and biased to some extent. If the therapist does not assume this, but absolutizes his own perception and understanding, he will automatically dominate the patient by his own subjectivity, a danger against which Sartre warned.

In concluding this chapter we can do no better than to refer back to the example of Dr. Ramirez given at the beginning, and to repeat that there are arising in a number of corners demonstrations that the contribution of the cultural movement called existentialism to psychology and psychotherapy is indeed significant. This influence does and will appear in many guises, under different terms—and this is as it should be. Existentialism is an attitude toward the human existence which permeates almost every aspect of modern culture. That it should be content not to be a new school but to be a "gadfly" and a leaven in the loaf (to mix our figures) for psychotherapy, is in itself a demonstration of the only genuinely existential attitude.

CONTRIBUTORS

PHILIP P. HALLIE is Professor of Philosophy at Wesleyan University, Middletown, Connecticut. Educated at Oxford (B. Litt.) and at Harvard (Ph.D), he taught at Vanderbilt University prior to taking his present position. He has been a Guggenheim Fellow in Paris (1958–59) and an American Council of Learned Societies Fellow in London (1966–67). He represented the United States at the International Institute of Philosophy meetings in Mysore, India, in 1959. He is the author of *Maine de Biran* and *Montaigne and Personal Philosophy*, and editor of *Scepticism, Man, and God*. His essays have appeared in *Mind, Journal of Philosophy, Philosophical Quarterly*, and *The Encyclopedia of Philosophy*.

ROGER L. SHINN is Professor of Applied Christianity and Dean of Instruction at Union Theological Seminary and

Adjunct Professor of Religion at Columbia University in New York. He studied at Heidelberg College (A.B.), Union Theological Seminary (B.D.), and Columbia University (Ph.D.). His books include *Christianity and the Problem of History, The Existentialist Posture, Tangled World,* and *Man: The New Humanism.* He was writer and narrator of the television series, *Tangled World.* He has lectured at many colleges and universities. He is a member of the editorial board of *Christianity and Crisis* and a contributor to numerous journals and periodicals.

STANLEY ROMAINE HOPPER, formerly Dean of the Graduate School and Professor of Philosophy and Letters at Drew University, is Professor of Religion at Syracuse University. His studies were at the University of Southern California (A.B.), Boston University School of Theology (B.D.), Harvard University, the University of Zurich, Mansfield College (Oxford, England), and Drew (Ph.D.). He is the author of *The Crisis of Faith,* editor of *Spiritual Problems in Contemporary Literature,* editor (with David L. Miller) of *Interpretation: The Poetry of Meaning,* and a contributor to many other books. He has taught a course in "Religion and Modern Literature," presented over WCBS-TV. He was an American delegate to the First Conference on Christianity and Art at the Chateau de Bossey, Switzerland, and he is President of the Foundation for the Arts, Religion and Culture.

ROGER ORTMAYER, after teaching at Mount Union College and at Southern Methodist University, became Director of the Department of Church and Culture of the National Council of Churches. He studied at Dakota Wesleyan University (A.B.), Garrett Theological Seminary (B.D.), Northwestern University (M.A.), the University of Chicago, and Western Reserve University. From 1950 to 1958 he was editor of *motive* magazine, which has been described as the most effective single influence in introducing American college students to contemporary art. He is author of *Worship and the Arts,* of numerous essays, and of dramatic, television, and motion-picture scripts. He has traveled around the world in his studies of art, doing research especially in Europe and in Turkey.

ROLLO MAY, psychoanalyst, is Supervisory and Training Analyst at the William Alanson White Institute of Psychiatry, Psychology and Psychoanalysis in New York. He studied at Oberlin College (A.B.) and Columbia University (Ph.D.). He has taught or counseled at American College (Salonika, Greece), Michigan State University, College of the City of New York, New York University, Harvard University, and the New School for Social Research. He has lectured widely at other colleges and universities. He has written *Art of Counseling, The Meaning of Anxiety,* and *Man's Search for Himself;* and he has edited *Existence: A New Dimension in Psychiatry* and *Psychology and Symbolism in Religion and Literature.* He is author of many essays and scientific papers.

INDEX

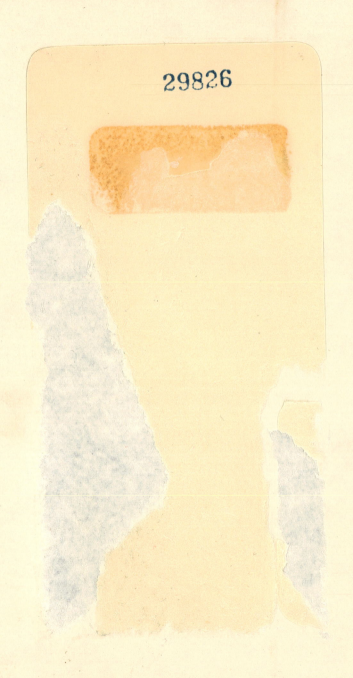

29826